The Out of Towner's Guide Book to Happy Valley, NC

by
James Houston Groome

Love you, Aunt Dot!
Leila

Edited by Leila M. McMichael

keela0047@gmail.com

Written in Lenoir, NC by James Houston Groome. June 2019.

ISBN 9781072088486

Dedication

This book is dedicated to all the fine folks, and my friends, of Happy Valley and their ancestors who helped build a community based on tradition, love and the creative spirit.

The Valley forever!

"There is something about jumping a horse over a fence, something that makes you feel good. Perhaps it's the risk, the gamble. In any event, it's a thing I need."

-- William Faulkner

Table of Contents

Prologue

This book contains some of my personal recollections as well as little known facts, general knowledge, and a lot of humor. As such it is autobiographical in places, but not an autobiography.

The information in this book is about, but not limited to Happy Valley in North Carolina -- which I call "the Valley" -- to which I refer to the entire general region which is found in the upper end of the Yadkin-Pee Dee River Basin, home to the Yadkin River and its headwaters. The Yadkin flows northeast from Caldwell County into Wilkes County and beyond before turning south to the ocean.

To be specific, there is also a community of Happy Valley, NC, which is a very populated locale within the Township of Patterson in Caldwell County. This has confused some as to the location of HISTORIC Happy Valley which I discuss in the section on "Historic Places." There is also a small locale called Patterson in the Township of Patterson. Though Patterson and Happy Valley communities are both in the Township of Patterson, they are also part of Lenoir. But because they were originally separate communities, back in the day there were letters sent simply addressed to "Patterson, NC" and "Happy Valley, NC." And they were delivered!

Another example of how place names can develop is a personal one. A lot of my early Groome relatives settled in an area near Greensboro, NC in the township of Sumner. So, the community was called Groometown. The Groometown Road in Greensboro is named after them and runs for 7 or 8 miles south from Greensboro passing through Groometown.

Historic Happy Valley as a geographical area is pretty big, running for about 28 miles west to east. Back in the day, the west end of Happy Valley was called Upper Happy Valley and the east end was called Lower Happy Valley, which is nowadays called Yadkin Valley. It's hard to tell what the exact population of historic Happy Valley is, but it's at least several thousand. The Yadkin River winds through the Valley, which is very wide, flat and beautiful. Just before exiting Happy Valley, it ends in beautiful Kerr Scott Reservoir which has many recreational opportunities. There are 24 "Historic Happy Valley" milepost signs along scenic Hwy 268 from Caldwell County to Wilkes County.

In the past people have asked me what are some of my most favorite things that I've done in Happy Valley. Some of my earliest enjoyable experiences in the Valley were when I was in the Boy Scouts of America and we used to camp in the nut grove at Fort Defiance (where the original fort itself once was). My friendships with people at Patterson School, while I was still in high school, are also fond memories. I had a little experience with boarding schools, having gone to one in Virginia for a year. It was interesting to see how others dealt with life at theirs.

Some of the Gothic and other alternative music that I'm into today stemmed from some of those friendships I made at the Patterson School, but I did not go to school there. After hearing recordings of the vocal stylings of singers like Elizabeth Fraser and Peter Murphy of the United Kingdom, a lot of music that I had heard in the past sounded kind of plain in comparison. I am still interested in their music and I cover some of their material. These musicians made quite an impression on me. I discovered Fraser and Murphy ironically in the Valley.

Later still as a young man, I took part in sweat lodges in the late 90's and had great Medieval and Renaissance cultural learning experiences in the SCA at

Fort Defiance. The SCA, or Society for Creative Anachronism, is a Medieval and Renaissance recreation society that started in the 1960's. I also enjoyed living in Happy Valley by the river with my then-wife, Sandra Renee Greer Groome. She had formerly lived in Beacon Hills in the Valley. While I was married, we lived in town, then some later at River Run Ranch in the Valley. When I moved back to Lenoir, I often traveled back to the Valley to perform at large, titled house parties such as many of the various "Flatwood Stocks."

Also, musically speaking, I was in the Valley when I first heard William Jackson (he is a Scottish harper) and Grainne Hambly (she is an Irish harper) perform their beautiful Celtic music live. For those who did not know, a harper plays Celtic traditional music; a harpist plays classical music.

The Yadkin River winds through and crisscrosses Happy Valley. I have had fun on both the north and the south sides of the river. Many people have had so much fun in the Valley, they dubbed it "Happnin' Valley!"

And, of course, fishing in the Yadkin river is also included in my favorite times in Happy Valley. The middle of the river is a state-owned, neutral area, from what I gather, and it's partially why, for example, people will "walk" the river occasionally in some areas while fishing. But they still have to keep moving basically. I myself have tried to do that a few times with both a regular rod and reel and a fly rod, which made for difficult hang-ups because the Little Yadkin River in the Valley is often heavily canopied.

I met Jimmy McAteer while we were at Hibriten High School. Only decades later were we reunited by the fact that he is Sandra's nephew. We often fished together on his old land and land that once belonged to Sandra's brother, Reggie, and his wife, Sonja, along the Yadkin River. There was many a "Hey, y'all, wa'chis!" moments between us in the Valley.

Good times!

James H. Groome

9

Here's a beautiful piece of Happy Valley at my newest home in Lenoir. It was given to me by friend, and ex-brother-in-law, Reggie. It was from his old place out at River Run Ranch when he lived there, and where I stayed occasionally. It is very spiritual to me.

This photo of Happy Valley, near where I used to live, is an image I most associate with the region.

Map

HISTORIC HAPPY VALLEY

1 - **Beginning of Historic Happy Valley** starts at the intersection of Hwy 268 and Starr Road 1460 (Yadkin River Road) at bridge over Yadkin River. Ending point for upper portion of Happy Valley Greenway which starts at the parking lot of the Happy Valley Ruritan Club, near the Happy Valley Elementary School. Across the bridge is the starting point for the lower portion of the Greenway which begins at the lower parking lot near the Hill Billy Trading Post and ends at a small park with a flagpole. All walkers must retrace steps back to each respective parking lot.

2 - **First Historic Happy Valley Mile Marker #1**

3 - **Chapel of Rest** (Civil War hero Collett Leventhorpe buried here)

4 - **Patterson Science Center** (formerly Patterson School and Patterson School for Boys) near Historic Happy Valley mile marker #3

5 - **Fort Defiance** (Revolutionary War hero William Lenoir buried here)

6 - **Laura Foster's Grave and Memorial Marker.** Happy Valley Fiddlers Convention held a few hundred feet east (near Historic Happy Valley mile marker #9)

7 - **Tom Dooley's Grave** (off Tom Dula Rd. near Historic Happy Valley mile marker #15 and state historic marker)

8 - **Ferguson, NC** (where one of Daniel Boone's cabins was found)

9 - **Whippoorwill Village** (with reconstructed Daniel Boone cabin and other historic buildings)

10 - **Kerr Scott Reservoir** (where another of Daniel Boone's cabins is under water)

11 - **Final Historic Happy Valley mile marker #24** (just ¼ mile from Reservoir Rd which crosses Kerr Scott Dam)

OMVT - Overmountain Victory Trail Sites. The Surry County Patriot Militia departed Elkin, NC approximately September 27, 1780. They camped at Tory Oak in Wilkesboro on September 27, 1780. Then they camped approximately two miles west of Tom Dooley's Grave along the Yadkin River on September 28, 1780. Finally, they camped at Fort Crider in Lenoir on September 29, 1780. From there they continued on their way to Morganton, NC. where they met up with the OVT group out of Abingdon, VA and headed south to Kings Mountain to do battle with General Ferguson, defeating him and his forces

CW - Civil War Sites.
Burning of Patterson Mill by General Gillman, one of Stoneman's Raiders

Foreword to Language

Hello! For generations Happy Valley and many other places in the Appalachia mountains, hills, and valleys, have had a wealth of unique pronunciations, vernacular expressions, old-timey sayings, and colloquialisms, etc. Many one syllable words must be pronounced as two syllables and the tone of voice can't always be expressed or conveyed correctly when read, however, I have attempted to convey it to the best of my ability here.

Pronunciation of common words with a mountain accent or Appalachian accent is key to fitting in with the locals. For example, "Appalachian" is NOT pronounced Appa-LAY-shun; it's pronounced, AppaLATCH-an.

In writing and re-writing this book, I've been forced to notice a phenomenon that I seem to keep doing and that's choosing to use the mountain spelling of "Ya'll" with the apostrophe between the "a" and the "l " instead of "Y'all" with the apostrophe between the "y" and "a." It's probably the most widely used contraction around here and both sound the same.

I've been writing and using "Ya'll" with the apostrophe between the "a" and the "l" for years. I suppose the other way is more "correct," but it's hard to get out of the habit. Mountain linguists could probably argue for it either way. Formal writers argue strongly for "y'all" as being more correct. So, I will force myself to spell it more "correctly," still... if I slip, ya'll understand, right?

Those spellings and phonetic pronunciations I've mentioned here aren't meant to mock, as I myself have used a lot of these expressions and pronunciations, especially since I was raised in the King's Creek area, about 9 miles from Happy Valley as the crow flies. They are simply meant to amuse and even educate in some instances. I'm sure I've left out many good ones but enjoy the rich collection I've managed to remember!

James H. Groome

CHAPTER 1
Language

WORDS (PRONUNCIATIONS)

Words (Pronunciation)	Sentence (How it's said or sounded in the Valley and elsewhere locally)
Back there (Bak air)	Get back there! (Git bak air)
Bag (byagh)	Bag is another word for poke. (Byagh is another werd fer poke)
Cat (ca-yit)	You better bring in all your cats. (Y'better bring in all yer ca-yits)
Crawdad (Crawl dad)	A crawdad bit my big toe! (A crawl dad bit my big toe)
Dog (Dawg)	That dog will bite you! (Dat dawg'll bite you!)
Gas (guyce)	I got to get gas for the tractor. (I gotta get guyce fer da tractor)
Grits (gree-its)	These are grits. (Em'er gree-its)
In (ee-an)	Come in the house. (Come ee-an th' house)
Listen (lee-a-son)	I want you to listen! (I won't you to lee-a-son)
Lord (lowered)	Oh Lord have mercy, what now?! (O lowered have mercy, wut now?!)

13

Poison (pizen), poisonous (pizenus)	Don't eat that; it's poisonous. (Don't eat dat; it's pizenus)
Pretty (purdy)	That's a pretty strange cat. (Thayit's a purdy strange cayit)
That (thayit) (or sometimes dat)	That's right! (Thayit's write!)
Them (the-im) (or sometimes dem)	Them dogs are after the chickens again! (Dem dogs are after the chikkins agin)
There (thair) (used with that)	Somethings wrong with that child. (That thair youngin' ain't right)
Your (yer)	Your mama wants you. (Yer mama's hollerin' fer you)

COMMON WORDS & PHRASES

A piece = a ways to travel | I'm goin' up the road a piece.

A-fixin' = getting ready to | I'm a-fixin' to go to church.

Ain't = isn't | Ain't that your wife going there?

Anotherin' = another one | If you liked them biscuits,
git you'ns anotherin'.

Arthuritis = arthritis | She's got the Arthuritis in her hands.
Arthur = arthritis | Me and Arthur are gonna have to sit
down and have a talk today.

Ary = any | Is there ary a one left?

Cain't = don't | I cain't know which one to choose.

Carry me = take me | Will you carry me to the store?

Cheer = did you hear | Cheer a car comin'?

Diabeetus = diabetes | He got type two diabeetus.

Dinner = means lunch | I got to eat my dinner and go back
to work.

Dough sop = gravy | Pour me some dough sop on my biscuit!

Fair to middlin' = OK | Grandpa says he's been fair to middlin'.
(Phrase came from an average grade of cotton called "Fair to
middling."It has become an Southern expression meaning OK)

Flitter = type of flat pan bread | Dat mule mashed my toe flat as a flitter!

Get/got a-holt (varies by context) | Dem hornets got a-holt of him!

Git fiddle = guitar | Grandpa pulled out his git fiddle
and started playin'.

15

Good'un = good one	That apple was a good'un.
Grab a-holt = grab hold	Grab a-holt of dat youngin'!
Gumpy = lazy	That youngin' is gumpy!
Hainted = haunted	The old Hayes place is hainted!
Haints = haunts or ghosts	Ya'll ain't believin' in dem haints, are ye?
Hatefulest = most hateful	Dem are the hatefulest people!
Heatherns = heathens	Dem lil' heatherns runnin through the house made Granny ill.
Hep = Help	I cain't hep it if I still like her!
Hey = Hello	Hey y'all!
Holler = yell or call	I will give you a holler before I go.
Holler = small valley or hollow	She lives up in Brushy Holler.
Howdy = How do you do	Howdy, Brother Bob!
Idee = idea	I ain't got no idee!
Ill = angry, testy	He's ill as a hornet!
Ill = sick	My granny's took ill.
Jeet = did you eat	Come in! Jeet?
Kindly = kind of	I kindly spent too much at the store.
Learnt = learned	It ain't learnt him nuthin'!
Liked = almost	He liked to slip down that whole bank!
Li'kis = like this	I tole dat city slicker, "Dat ain't how you hoe! Do it li'kis!"

16

Lyin' ya = lying to you	I ain't lyin' ya!
Mater(s) = tomato(es)	Dem maters done rotted on the vine.
Meaner'n = meaner than	She's meaner'n hell!
Mess = hand full	He's a mess.
Mess = large quantity	I fixed me a good ole mess of creecy greens last night.
Might'n = might	If you set yer beer down, might'n it spill?
Mom an'em = mother and relatives	How's yer mom an'em?
MOUNTAIN mean = very mean	Dem peoples up air is MOUNTAIN mean.
Nary = not	Nope, there's nary a one left.
Pert near = almost	His momma pert near killed him for kissing his sister.
Pickin' (varies by context)	Pickin' cotton by day; pickin' the guitar by night!
Real quick like = very fast	Her daddy came home so he got outta there real quick like.
Reckon = guess	I reckon I'll be late fer work.
Rite'dar = right there	Put it rite'dar.
Ruint = ruined	The dog jumped on the table; now supper's ruint!
S'geet = let's go eat	I'm hongry! S'geet.
Sorry = extremely poor	He's a sorry excuse for a husband.

Stove up = stiff and sore	He dug taters all day, now he's all stove up.
Strangs = strings	Yer git fiddle needs new strangs!
(The) Sugar = diabetes	She's got the sugar. He's got sugar real bad.
Supper = evening meal	Go wash your hands; it's time for supper.
Up'air = up there	De law's up'air!
Waspers = wasps	Dem waspers got a hold of him!
White lightnin' = Moonshine, Corn liquor, "panther pee"	He got pulled with a trunk full o' white lightnin'!"
Y'all = All of you (sometimes written ya'll)	See y'all later!
Y'all's = All of your	It's y'all's problem.
You'ns / Yinz (yinz) = All of you	You'ns is crazy. Yinz be purdy!.
Yonder = where you are not	Go up yonder! Over yonder! Fine then, go down yonder!
Yo'nt = you want	Yo'nt to go to town?
Young'ins = children	Them dar youngins is gonna git kicked for messin' with dat mule!
Y'ought not = you shouldn't	Y'ought not let dem youngins out dare in dat damn road! Y'ought not talk to yer momma like at!
Your'n (can sound like "your-in")	Your'n trouble!
Yourn (can sound like "urine:)	That beer's yourn. (singular possessive)
Yourn's (plural possessive)	These gravy biscuits are yourn's.
Yournses (also plural possessive)	Them pigs is yournses.

SOOTHING SOUTHERNISMS

Terms of endearment, such as honey, darlin', sunshine, sweetheart, and the like, may be randomly added to soften the harshness of any comment.

Go wash yer face! You look like you been suckin' on a sow…darlin'.

Also saying, "I love you, but…" is a standard preface to soften a harsh statement.

I love you, but you stink to high heaven.

You can also say "Bless his or her heart" after any put down or brutally honest observation to make it all right.

"She's a briar patch (<u>blank</u>), bless her heart!"

"Bless it!" -- The one comforting phrase that covers all situations –

"I stumped my toe!!!" Reply: "Bless it!"

A short form of "Bless it" is to simply say "Bless!"

COMMON EXPRESSIONS

"Them are some eatin' **people**!" -- Those people eat a lot.

"He's meaner'n a red-striped snake!" -- When you describe people, you can use animals as an analogy.

"It's hotter'n a goat's butt in a pepper patch." -- Animals can be used to describe situations as well.

"It's Katy, bar the door!" -- There's going to be trouble

"Yinz be purdy!" or "Y'all be purdy!"
> (a phrase I learned while living in Kings Creek) --
> > You all behave.
> (or in some cases, you all be pretty!)

"I thought youn's went down to your raft, but never made it." -- I don't want you here.

"Don't be ugly!" -- Don't be mean.

"Everybody and his brother knows he cheated on her." -- Everyone knows he cheated on her.

"It's enough to puke a dog off a gut wagon!" -- It's enough to make me vomit.

"She's finer en frog's hair!" -- She's fine looking.

"What a LOOKIN' thing!" -- What a shocking looking thing.

"I'm a stomp his butt!" -- I'm going to beat him up.

"I wasn't afeared." -- I wasn't afraid.

"Come in for a spell!" -- Come in and stay a while.

"Grits is groceries." -- Grits are a staple.

"Well, corn's in the field…" -- suggestion from one spouse to another to get romantic or the work's done, time to relax

"It's too wet to plow." -- Plowing or any kind of work isn't going to get done at the moment.

"God willing, and the creeks don't rise." -- Unless something unforeseen happens, such and such will get done –
>"I'll be there tomorrow, God willing
>and the creeks don't rise!"

"That girl can talk the ears off a billy goat!" -- That girl talks a lot

"Emerson good-uns." -- Those are some good ones.

Another couple of other sayings, locally in Caldwell County that I've heard, when asked how you are doing, are:

>"Well, I was alright, but I got over it."

Not sure what it means, but I love it and use it. Could mean one should be more grateful than just "alright." Could mean something happened to ruin your day. I guess it depends on why you are saying it.

>"Well, any day above ground is a good day."
>Means I'm grateful to be alive.

CHAPTER 2
Culture

Southern Colloquials

I wear the hand-me-down countenance of my
Grandfather like an old pea coat in winter.
Eloquent voices of the South like:
I'm sick as a yellow dog.
Grits is South Carolina ice cream.
He is strong as a white mule
And up-to-par and
Katy bar
Embellish my stride.

My children will fit snug into these anthems.
They'll know that if you cut the head off of a
Snapping turtle and nail it to an old tree and
Touch a pair of pliers to its beak,
It will snap it out of your hand and won't let go
'Til lightning strikes.

Let the thunder and lightning haunt the Southern
Sky, so I can use the pliers again to fix the
Closed-faced reel for tomorrow, I will go to the
Pond and hope a dragonfly lands on my rod to
Rest.

James H. Groome

My poem won 1st place in the Caldwell County Literary competition in the
Poetry category in 1998.

Regarding dyeing with natural dyes: even the green husks of a black walnut can be used to dye cloth brown. You don't have to just use dark ones. I saw this demonstrated by an SCA friend in the Valley one time. There's lots more information on the internet about plants that can be used to dye cloth naturally.

Moonshine, historically an illegally brewed alcohol from corn by mountain folk, is also called white lightning, corn liquor and panther pee. If you keep going through Happy Valley, you'll end up in Wilkesboro, the most famous origins of "moonshine running" (corn liquor) in the world. Even though the Internal Revenue Service ("Revenooers") did their best to stem the tide of illegal alcohol, it was North Carolina ABC stores that put most moonshiners out of business because of the low cost, variety and availability of legal liquor, including "moonshine." However, illegal stills are still in operation today and one in Wilkes County was destroyed as recently as January 2018. Here's a still display from the Wilkes Heritage Museum.

Prospecting has also been a popular hobby in the Valley. Up until the Gold Rush of 1849, North Carolina was the leading gold state. Even today our mountains are riddled with abandoned gold mines and prospectors still "explore" the Yadkin River in the Valley occasionally for gold.

Plantain

"Legend has it that Alexander the Great discovered it and brought it with him back to Europe in 327 BCE. It has been referred to as the Whiteman's Foot by Native Americans, as wherever they went, it seemed to spring up. And in some places, it is seen as a noxious, invasive weed. It is, however, a useful little plant. It has been used by many cultures the world over, and the Saxons considered it one of their nine sacred herbs." (Wells, 2019)

Younger leaves of the common broadleaf plantain are edible and can be used raw in salads. Some of its herbal uses include teas used for mouthwash, preventing sores in the mouth and taken for other internal ailments of the digestive system including heartburn. Native Americans found that the leaves could be used to relieve the pain of insect stings and bites. It was also effective on poison ivy and other rashes, as well as promoting healing of sores and bruises.

Even just chewing up or crushing the leaves and putting them on a wound as a poultice helped relieve pain and promoted healing. As with any herb or supplement, consult your physician before using plantain in any form.

Jewelweed

This beautiful herb that grows along branches and in moist soil, usually has orange flowers, sometimes yellow, can also be used for stings and bites, but is most commonly used for counteracting poison ivy and poison oak sap you may get exposed to. Also, something slightly more modern to counteract the effects from poison ivy is the scoopable cat litter that you can make into a paste. When smeared on, it will help draw the poison out.

Aloe Vera

My favorite to use on burns is aloe vera (Middle Eastern in origin), directly from the plant. It also aids in digestion. Aloe vera has a host of other healing properties, too numerous to go into here, but check it out on the internet. As always do a skin test first on any new use of an herb or any product.

Thyme

Some culinary herbs can have other uses. Thyme can not only be used for cooking but also has been used for centuries to treat a number of ailments including digestion and sore throats.

DISCLAIMER

There are literally thousands of Old Ways and remedies. I can't go into much more detail as this book is more of a potpourri of some things pertaining to Happy Valley and this general region of the Appalachians. One could write an entire book on just the Old Ways which covers a lot more than just remedies.

Advice during hard times?

I can tell you what a foreign friend, Mo, told me about 18 years ago: "Everything'll work out; it's the Southern way."

CHAPTER 3
Folklore

*Simple Divinations, Tips, and Clues on the World
around the Appalachian Resident
or*

"Did Y'all Know Thayit?"

Rubbing a sage leaf over your teeth every day can help whiten them.

Eating strawberries helps whiten teeth.

A half teaspoon of cinnamon a day helps your blood sugar maintenance.

You can use olive oil on zippers, skin and hair.

After you wash your dawg, if she still smells like dawg, you can rub some fresh picked rosemary on her coat.

Dinner is served around noon, incorrectly called "lunch" by non-mountain folks.

Supper is our evening meal, incorrectly called "dinner" by non-mountain folks.

When it rains while the sun is shining, the Devil is beating his wife.

Wooly worms can be used to predict the kind of winter coming. A mostly black worm with only its front and hind ends brown means a long winter.

When the black walnuts start falling off early, it's a sign of a long winter coming.

If a snapping turtle bites you, it won't turn loose until it thunders (or in some cases, lightning).

"The fish are bitin' if the cows are grazin'."

"The leaves are turnin' upside down on the trees. This means a storm be comin'."

"Storms'll run that river!" -- Storms tend to follow a river's course

"Heat lightning" -- Is often pointed out in the distance on a hot, humid night. A panorama of clouds flicker, but there's no thunder. Heat lighting is an old wives' tale. The clouds light up from normal lightning produced by a thunderstorm that's too far away for you to hear the thunder or see the lightning.

"Rolling thunder" -- Rolling thunder, memorialized by a popular gospel song, is usually the result of an extensive bolt of lightning that creates thunder at each end with several seconds between striking the ground. Also, the sound of a lightning strike can bounce off nearby clouds to creating a kind of echo resulting in a rumbling sound.

> *It's much more vivid to experience some of these things in Happy Valley because the Valley has few streetlights and the skies can be brilliant.   JHG*

"Persimmons aren't fit to eat until the frost bites 'em." -- Not true; frost has no effect on the ripening of persimmons, but the fruit tends to ripen very late in the fall, so frost has been associated with this.

Putting a dryer sheet in your hat while you're fishing can help cut down on insect bites. Also, "dry rubbing" an orange peel or rosemary on your head and neck has been known to ward off biting pests.

WHEN TO PLANT

Being a farmer meant working the land almost year round. It wasn't limited to the spring, summer and fall months. In the winter months, there was farming work to be done. Sometimes this included burning a field to enrich the soil and prepare it for planting. It meant planting and tending winter crops, pruning, and plowing and fertilizing ground in preparation for the spring when the most planting would occur.

How did the farmers know when to plant? In the Appalachians, most farmers used March as a general rule of thumb as to the start of Spring, but they also knew that in their mountains, frosts and cold weather could continue nearly into early summer; however, cold tolerant crops could be planted.

Farmers back in the day often used signs from nature to determine when to plant. These included observing the wild plants and animals around them, weather signs, phases of the moon, and in some cases even astrological data. There is a famous song that says, "by the dark of the moon I planted," and this refers to the practice of planting vegetables that grow beneath the ground when the moon is waning or new (dark). Conversely, plants that grew above the ground were to be planted when the moon was waxing or full.

Almanacs and planting calendars were often used. Almanacs were especially helpful in telling the farmer the phases of the moon and the astrological signs so important to their planting practices. Planting was usually done with all signs aligned for a positive result. Today there are almanac calendars put out by certain businesses that contain this old timey information. Here is a small section of the Boone (NC) Drugs Inc. calendar for April 2019. Not only does it tell you the dates when to plant the above ground crops, the root crops and the seed crops, it also tells you when the fishing is best!

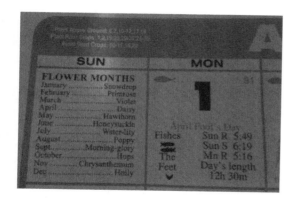

Zodiac signs were also used to differentiate days in an almanac and these were significant in determining planting schedules. These signs lasted two or three days in sequence, allowing for planting to take place during that time. The Zodiac signs are: Aries, Taurus, Gemini, Cancer, Leo, Virgo, Libra, Scorpio, Sagittarius, Capricorn, Aquarius and Pisces. Planting was usually done when days were in "the neck" (Bull or Taurus), "the breast" (Crab or Cancer), "the loins" (Scorpion or Scorpio), and "the feet" (Fishes or Pisces), although there was some divergence. The 12 Zodiac signs repeated in order sequentially and were followed throughout the growing season.

Also used were signs from nature. Corn was supposed to be planted after the first whippoorwill call, and some use that as the signal to plant tomatoes. Sometimes specific days were used to plant crops. Some folks plant potatoes on Good Friday. According to the National Park Service website, under the topic Great Smokey Mountains "Planting," some farmers would plant turnips on Ascension Day (40 days after Easter), to insure a better crop.

Other plant lore from the National Park Service website are:

• Red-headed persons have the best luck with peppers.
• If cucumbers are planted on Saturday, they will be bitter.
• If you plant cucumbers in the full moon, they will all run to vines, and will not bear.
• If you laugh while planting corn, the grains will fall apart on the cob. ("Great Smokey Mountains: Planting." July 1, 2015)

"HAINTINGS"

Stories of ghosts abound in North Carolina. Happy Valley, and the area around it, has its share! If you want to read a good book about North Carolina ghosts, check out *Appalachian Ghosts* by Nancy Roberts and R. G. Absher's *Ghosts of the Yadkin Valley* for more local stories. I have a few stories I want to share with you that I know about or have heard about.

Years ago, a friend of mine who had some family from the Sampson area (about 20 miles from upper Happy Valley past Buffalo Cove, which is part in Caldwell County and part in Wilkes County), took me up to a haunted area in the woods there. It was an abandoned road, specifically a sharp bend on that road, where people have heard the rolling or creaking sound of wagon wheels from covered wagons or old farm wagons still traveling that road. We listened for a long time, but we heard nothing. The locals still maintain that area as being haunted.

Another area in the woods that is haunted is Brown Mountain in Burke County to the west of historic Happy Valley. For hundreds of years, mysterious lights have been seen there. No one knows what causes these lights, but they have been investigated by government agencies and others for years. Now there are a lot of photographs and Youtube videos of the lights online, so you don't have to go there to see what's going on.

Some say it's the spirit of a faithful slave looking for his lost master. Others say they're lights from a search party looking for a murdered woman. Some say the lights are from Indian women looking for the bodies of their loved ones that fell in the battle between the Catawba and Cherokee back in 1737.

In the Music section of this book, I talk about the Brown Mountain lights a bit more and the song inspired by them, but I wanted to mention them here because some people say restless spirits cause these lights.

The Chapel of Rest in upper Happy Valley is also the site of some possible hauntings. On the "Ghosts of America" website, there is an area called "Lenoir, North Carolina Ghost Pictures." Someone posted a picture taken of one of the windows at the Chapel of Rest which shows what looks like a female figure inside the Chapel. This picture was taken some years ago, the person said.

Another story of the Chapel of Rest goes like this. A married preacher there had an affair with a woman in the congregation. Somehow the wife found out and then the congregation found out. He supposedly went to the Chapel of Rest and shot and killed himself. There is a dark stain on the floor of the chapel and some say it was where his blood stained the floor. Others say that it was where the old wood stove sat and discolored the floor. There have been no sightings of the ghost of the preacher, but no one has been able to remove the stain.

The Patterson School is also the site of a haunting in upper Happy Valley. Before it was co-educational, it was the Patterson School for Boys. There was a lady who worked as a babysitter for the Headmaster there, a Miss Pinkney. She always wore a full-length black pinafore dress. She did not like some changes at Patterson School for Boys, possibly when the institution went co-educational, but it is not known for sure. What is known is that she was unhappy about some change there and when she died, she began to haunt the school. Her figure, still dressed in her black pinafore, was seen looking out of the window of one of the buildings at Patterson School. Another person believes they saw her as well.

The story of Miss Pinkney was told to us by Mrs. Loretta Melton Hartley of Happy Valley. She states that she is related to Ann Melton who, along with Tom C. Dula, was accused of the murder of Laura Foster. Ann Melton was later acquitted and Tom Dula was hung. There have been many ghostly occurrences related to the story of Tom Dooley, and Mrs. Hartley had a couple to share

She said that her son was coming back late one night from UNC-Greensboro on Hwy 268. He was listening to the radio and as he passed Laura Foster's

grave, the radio cut out and a strange voice came over the speakers trying to say something. It scared him to death, and he hurried home to relate the frightful experience to his family.

She also told of another incident where her brother was working outside his house about 1 1/2 miles past Laura Foster's grave. A stranger stopped to tell him something. He said that he was coming towards the location of the grave and something told him to stop. So, he did and went to the grave out in the field.

When he got there, he heard a woman's voice say, "This is not where I'm buried. I am on German Hill." Interestingly, I did come across a source that mentioned that Laura Foster's family lived in the community of German Hill in Caldwell County at the time of her murder.

In a newspaper article from the *Winston-Salem Journal* dated October 22, 2009, journalist Monte Mitchell reveals that the old Wilkes jailhouse (just a little to the east of lower historic Happy Valley) where Tom Dooley and Ann Melton were imprisoned may also be haunted.

According to R. G. Absher, a local historian and author of *Ghosts of the Yadkin Valley*, some former employees have stated that on cloudy, dreary days they could hear what sounded like people scuffling and sounds of a man and a woman quarreling. Other sources report footsteps.

For those of you who are ghost hunters, the article also has an interesting insert article by *Hickory Daily Record* reporter, Ragan Robinson, on ghost hunting "Tools of the Trade."

Wilkesboro itself is a supernatural goldmine. The Wilkes Heritage Museum conducts regular Candlelight Ghost Tours and all you have to do is contact them to arrange a tour and maybe experience the paranormal for yourself.

Tom Dula's state historical marker is found at the intersection of Hwy 268 and Tom Dula Rd. and is near Historic Happy Valley mile marker #15.

According to the North Carolina Visitor Center website, Tom Dooley was buried in a cemetery in lower Happy Valley near Elksville, NC which is about 2 miles west of Ferguson, NC in Wilkes County.

Interesting enough, though Tom Dula's grave is marked, there are no other markers there. So, they brought in a Ground Penetrating Radar (GPR) to see where the unmarked graves were and they found about 25 other sites, some male and some female. They are flagged on the site.

It is not known why there were no other markers, possibly this was because the people buried there were very poor and could not afford markers. It could be that this is the final resting place of the Dula branch that Tom is related to. They were less well-to-do than other Dulas in the area. The cemetery is called the Tom Dooley Cemetery.

Whippoorwill Academy and Village is a nearby outdoor museum in Ferguson, NC. It is operated by Margaret Carter Martine, the daughter of my high school art teacher, Edith Carter. Whippoorwill Academy and Village contains historic buildings, including a blacksmith shop, a church and other structures. The Tom Dooley Art Museum is there and contains paintings, photographs, and recounts from the legend.

The whole area is apparently haunted.

Under the section titled "Whippoorwill Academy and Village" on the North Carolina Visitor Center website, we learn that, "The grave of Tom Dooley is very near and some have even claimed to have seen Tom himself haunting the hillside." (Lee, 2013)

So, footsteps, scuffling, voices, and now even ghostly manifestations of Tom Dooley himself all add to the Happy Valley area paranormal folklore.

Last, but not least, I have been made aware of another haunted place in Happy Valley, none other than the Hill Billy Trading Post which is found at the beginning of the Yadkin Trail Greenway at the intersection of Hwy. 268 and the Yadkin River Road. The ghost of Mr. Woods, the former owner, has been seen on the premises. The first appearance was a full-body apparition of a grey-haired older man dressed in brown work coveralls. His son verified that it sounded like his father.

Mr. Woods has been seen a couple times since, but he is content to just appear and disappear at random. Once when Nona, the proprietor, left a pair of shoes in a chair and had to go talk to a customer, she returned to find the shoes perfectly placed on the floor in front of the chair. She knows she did not put the shoes there. When asked what the ghost was trying to tell her, she replied, "We don't put shoes in chairs." Nona and the ladies are comfortable sharing the Hill Billy Trading Post with Mr. Woods.

I am sure there are many more ghost stories out there that are yet untold. Maybe a book needs to be written called Haunted Happy Valley! In the meantime, be sure to check out the two books I mentioned for more bone-chilling stories of area "haintings."

Of note, there is an annual outdoor drama about Tom Dooley story called "Tom Dooley: A Wilkes County Legend." It is performed in mid-July at the Forest's Edge Amphitheater off Hwy 421 North in Historic Fort Hamby Park at 1534 South Recreation Road in Wilkesboro, NC.

You can obtain more information and sign up for show updates by going to the Bleu Moon Productions website at

https://www.bleumoonproductions.com/tom-dooley.html

CHAPTER 4
Historic Places

"Look Martha, mountains...."

"The Blue Ridge Mountains are a physiographic province of the larger Appalachian Mountains range. The mountain range is located in the eastern United States and extends 550 miles southwest from southern Pennsylvania through Maryland, West Virginia, Virginia, North Carolina, South Carolina, Tennessee and Georgia." ("Blue Ridge Mountains," 2019)

Happy Valley is nestled in the Blue Ridge Mountains and foothills. The Appalachian Mountain range is an older mountain range compared to the Rockies. Some of these mountains could be the oldest in the world. Yet we still have minor earthquakes. Our hills and valleys are gently covered with tall trees and rich vegetations, with rare outcroppings of bare rock. Happy Valley has been here for a long time.

When I talk about the Valley, I refer not only to the western or upper end that I lived in, but also to the entire HISTORIC Happy Valley region which has slowly been reduced over the years to a much smaller version of itself.

Historic Happy Valley stretches from Caldwell County into Wilkes County, specifically from the bridge at the intersection of the Yadkin River Road (State Road 1560) and Hwy. 268 in Caldwell County all the way to Kerr Scott Dam in Wilkes County, a length of about 28 miles.

The presence of twenty-four Historic Happy Valley mile markers, a project conceived in 2005 with markers installed in 2008 from a grant from the North Carolina State Arts Council, was the result of much research and documentation on the part of the Caldwell Arts Council.

It's time historic Happy Valley took back its proud heritage and this book hopes to help with that process.

Paleo Indians

Little is known about ancient Native Americans (Paleo Indians or Paleoamericans) in the Valley. They were nomadic, leaving little trace of their existence. Sources say the earliest known tribes are the Cherokee and Siouan Indians, also the Catawba, however these are Woodland culture Indians that appeared around 2000 BC. They are the ones who developed the bow and arrow hunting methods.

Spear heads (incorrectly called "arrowheads" which are usually an inch or less in length) from the Woodland culture tribes can still be found in plowed fields, many made of white quartz.

Little Yadkin River

Yadkin / Pee Dee River basin is the second largest river basin in the state of North Carolina. Sometimes called the "Little Yadkin River," the Yadkin River is the main body of water that flows through Happy Valley, but it is fed by different other smaller streams and branches. It is the seventh longest river in North Carolina.

In most of these waters they stock fish once a year, mainly trout.

Below is a view of the bridge at the intersection of Hwy 268 and Yadkin River Road where historic upper Happy Valley begins.

Fort Defiance

The "fort" at Fort Defiance, which is no longer there (only General William Lenoir's house and other structures remain), was initially constructed prior to the Revolutionary War (1775) to ward against Indian attacks. The house was built much later (1792), and in true Southern fashion, named after the original fort.

Probably one of my favorite nut groves is in the woods there at Fort Defiance, which was actually where the original fort once was. Epic Boy Scouts events have also ensued over the years at the site's property. I remember long cold nights in that grove in the woods with the Boy Scouts.

Fort Defiance has hosted (of course) their own Colonial events, including encampments, demos, etc. but they also host Civil War events and reenactments. As mentioned earlier, they have also hosted Society for Creative Anachronism events. I also remember our woods battle there when I was in the SCA.

Fort Defiance by Ken Thomas. Public Domain.

Fort Defiance offers tours of the building and grounds during certain times of the year. Contact them for more information. You will notice that nearly all of the chairs and tables inside the house are small. People back then were smaller than they are today apparently.

The General's Chestnut Tree

The old chestnut tree is on the outskirts of the greater nut grove. Some believe that General William Lenoir himself planted the tree because it's so big and beautiful. Some theorists also believe there is an underground spring that runs near the tree (heard that in 1998).

I've mostly always asked trees before I take something from them, being taught to be respectful about such things, but one day in the Valley I was too hasty, and a repercussion ensued. Now whether or not the tree itself actually did this to me, consciously or not, I don't know. But trees and forests do have ways to protect themselves.

Some of our group asked for (and were apparently given) permission to gather chestnuts, especially since we were going to cook and eat them. I got in too big of a hurry and forgot to ask (even though someone reminded me) and WHAM, my head hit a low, thick limb, hard. Talk about instant karma.

As old as the tree is, there are curvy parts of the lower limbs that sometimes seem to come out of nowhere, especially if you are already a little fatigued and I was, I remember. I had just participated in an SCA event called "Archery Faire." I can't be sure, but I think another member of our Shire also had an "accident" with the tree that day. Not sure if they had also offended the tree or not.

Needless to say, I have since been more polite and cautious around trees, for the most part. However, there was one incident 14 years later during an equinox celebration under a black walnut tree near the river at the other end of the Valley where I lived. I even had surgery as a result of it. It was a painful reminder.

Getting back to the General's chestnut tree, I also remember an experience from my youth with the tree. I was in the Boy Scouts and some of us scouts were throwing un-husked chestnuts at each other. As you know, the husks are very prickly. Some of the boys discovered that if you put a leather glove on, you could throw the chestnuts without hurting yourself, while inflicting maximum damage on your fellow scouts. Well, the Scout Masters soon found out and that battle came to a quick halt.

Fort Defiance Cemetery

For those who do not know, a graveyard is associated with a church, while a cemetery is a stand-alone burial site; however, the two words are commonly interchanged. The old cemetery at Fort Defiance is a revered landmark in this beautiful historical region, just as the graveyard at the Chapel of Rest is, and others like them throughout Happy Valley. Revolutionary war hero General William Lenoir is buried in the Fort Defiance Cemetery.

There are other historic burial sites in Happy Valley other than Fort Defiance. In this book I have mentioned the Chapel of Rest graveyard, Laura Foster's grave which stands by itself, and Tom

Dooley's grave which is the only marked grave in a cemetery of unmarked graves. Always be respectful when visiting these places of rest and just make sure you are not trespassing on private property, as some of them are semi-private anyway.

General William Lenoir

On October 7, 1780, then Captain William Lenoir led a company of men called the OverMountain Militia into South Carolina and helped beat the British Army. The Battle of Kings Mountain was a big turning point in favor of the colonists, as Major Patrick Ferguson and his loyalist militia were defeated. These "over mountain" men were heroes. The OverMountain Victory trail is named for their route. It was very big part of our Boy Scout troup's education.

Here is a picture of General William Lenoir. Public Domain

Here is a picture from Amazon.com of the first edition of Margaret Harper's book showing the Fort Defiance House and the only known silhouette of General Lenoir.

An interesting quote in Margaret Harper's book, *Fort Defiance and the General*, is:

"Captain Lenoir says, 'Colonel Ferguson had placed himself on the top of Kings Mountain the morning before the battle in a boasting manner he had proclaimed that he was king of that mountain.' " (page 18)

Here is a line art caricature of General Ferguson proclaiming himself king of the mountain by Leila McMichael.

General Lenoir made Colonel Ferguson eat those words. Later that morning at the Battle of Kings Mountain Ferguson lost both the battle and his life to the colonials.

By the way General Lenoir's great, great, great grandson, William B. Lenoir, was an MIT Professor and NASA astronaut. He visited the city of Lenoir, NC back when I was in the 7th or 8th grade at William Lenoir Middle school named after his family. We all got to meet him at the school.

Official portrait Astronaut William B. Lenoir. Public Domain

It was around this same time I started learning how to play the trumpet from my teacher, Ed Whitener. By the way, his father was Orin Whitener, my Scoutmaster. This is a prime example of connectivity and the interconnectedness between people in a small community.

The Patterson School

The Patterson School is located in upper Happy Valley on the former Palmyra Plantation, owned by Samuel L. Patterson. The property was bequeathed to be a school for boys, named after Patterson, but later became a co-educational institution.

"It is a special place that dates back thousands of years to the Native American use of the "Nickajack Trail" which extended from the Great Lakes to Florida and ran through Patterson. This early 'highway' resulted in numerous Native American sites, 'Indian Trees', mounds and relics, in and around the school property."

("The Patterson School Foundation: About Us," n.d.)

General William Lenoir was Samuel Patterson's great grandfather. When I attended West Caldwell High School, I had friends at the Patterson School which was co-educational at the time. One of those friends introduced me to some of my favorite music that I still enjoy and cover now, as mentioned before in the Prologue. My friend, Doug Davis, was a teacher there. He is also a noted local musician and visual artist, and is active in the Civil War Reenactments and events that are occasionally held at Fort Defiance.

In 1988 and 1989 I remember visiting the campus Bell Tower which a lot of us thought was pretty Gothic and sparked our imaginations. I also remember one time going home from visiting a friend there, that I got pulled in my Oldsmobile Cutlass for speeding. I was listening to "West of the Fields" by R.E.M. There was something about the night air -- I was fresh out of the Valley on the open road on Hwy 321 -- and the music made me feel ALIVE and heightened my senses enough to where my foot got heavy on the gas pedal. Then I saw the blue lights... "Son, do you know how fast you were going?"

I drove that Oldsmobile Cutlass often into Happy Valley when I was 17 and 18.

Chapel of Rest and the Chapel of Rest Graveyard

The Chapel of Rest graveyard is one of three very old historic burial locations. It is right behind the Chapel of Rest which served the Patterson School.

The others are the cemetery at Fort Defiance and one more graveyard on the left side of a nearby Episcopalian church. A famous personage in the Chapel of Rest graveyard is Confederate Brigadier General Collett Leventhorpe, originally from England.

Stoneman's Raid

In late March of 1865, Union General George Stoneman and his troops marched through western North Carolina, destroying businesses, bridges, and train tracks, in essence anything they could to weaken the Confederate economy. One of the main factories that was destroyed in the Lenoir area was the cotton mill in Patterson, NC. This plaque in Patterson, NC commemorates the event.

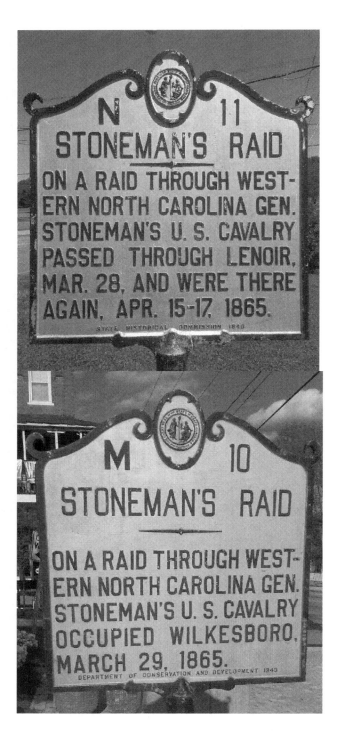

STONEMAN'S RAID

N 11

ON A RAID THROUGH WEST-
ERN NORTH CAROLINA GEN.
STONEMAN'S U. S. CAVALRY
PASSED THROUGH LENOIR,
MAR. 28, AND WERE THERE
AGAIN, APR. 15-17, 1865.

STATE HISTORICAL COMMISSION 1940

STONEMAN'S RAID

M 10

ON A RAID THROUGH WEST-
ERN NORTH CAROLINA GEN.
STONEMAN'S U. S. CAVALRY
OCCUPIED WILKESBORO,
MARCH 29, 1865.

DEPARTMENT OF CONSERVATION AND DEVELOPMENT 1940

Later during Easter weekend of that year, Stoneman and his men returned to Lenoir and rounded up 900 men and boys, including some wounded and sick Confederate soldiers, and imprisoned them at St. James Episcopal Church.

Laura Foster's Grave and The Legend of Tom Dooley

Laura Foster's grave is at one end of part of the Jones Farm. Happy Valley Fiddlers Convention meets there annually during the Labor Day weekend. I used to live across the river from it, as the crow flies, near there. The story goes that Laura Foster was stabbed by either her cousin Ann (Foster) Melton, or Tom Dooley and the most common reason was a lover's quarrel, but transmission of a venereal disease may have been involved.

Some Dula family descendants think that Tom was passed out drunk and Ann Melton took his knife and stabbed Laura Foster at that time. But in the end, Tom Dula confessed to the crime to save Ann Melton's life. Further discussion of Laura Foster and Tom Dooley is found in the Music section.

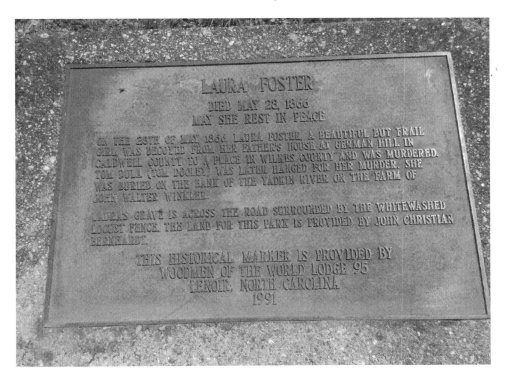

Daniel Boone

A discussion of Happy Valley would not be complete without mentioning America's most famous frontiersman, Daniel Boone. Daniel moved with his family to North Carolina in 1750. They settled in lower historic Happy Valley, now more commonly known as the Yadkin Valley area. Daniel was well known for his marksman's eye and he supported his family with his hunting skills even as a youngster. He met his future wife, Rebecca Bryan, there. They married circa 1753-1756 and began their own family in the Brushy Mountains of Wilkes County. The Brushy Mountain range runs through Happy Valley across five counties including Caldwell and Wilkes and includes Hibriten Mountain locally in Lenoir.

Daniel and his young family moved quite often living different places in Happy Valley, not surprising considering he is well known for his explorations and travels throughout his life. According to Dick Martine of Whippoorwill Village in Ferguson, NC, one of the cabins that they lived in is now underwater at the Kerr Scott Lake in Happy Valley and another one existed about 2 miles from Whippoorwill Village in Ferguson, NC. In tribute to Daniel Boone, Whippoorwill Village has reconstructed a cabin using the original fireplace and chimney gathered at that site.

His wife, Margaret Carter Martine (daughter of my former art teacher, Edith Carter), continued, "The Daniel Boone cabin at Whippoorwill is a reconstruction of his cabin from a description of Dr. William Spainhour (a Caldwell County dentist from the 1800's) who took measurements from the remains of Boone's cabin…. Also at Whippoorwill Academy and Village is a

1700's hunting lodge made of chestnut wood. This was originally located on a mountain in Watauga County and was a hunting cabin that Daniel Boone actually used when he was hunting up in the mountains."

So, Daniel Boone was very familiar with Happy Valley and the area around it. According to Randell Jones and the North Carolina Daniel Boone Heritage Trail, Inc. (2019), "From Elkville, a drive up Elk Creek ascends to the Blue Ridge Plateau on a route used by Daniel Boone on frequent hunting expeditions."

Daniel Boone and his family lived in North Carolina for over 20 years and then they moved to Kentucky. There are historic markers throughout North Carolina marking his trails and settlings, and many locations carry the Boone name in honor of him, including the city of Boone, NC, one of my favorite places to visit, in Watauga County.

Here is a marker in honoring him in Wilkesboro, NC.

Here is another marker in Wilkesboro put up by the Daughters of the American Revolution (DAR) honoring Daniel Boone.

The above plaque reads "Daniel Boone's Trail from North Carolina to Kentucky 1788. Marker by N. C. Daughters of the American Revolution"

Modern Landmarks

Yadkin Valley Grocery, aka "The Store" is a prominent local business in the western part of the Valley. You can report your caught fish there.

The Patterson Post Office is a landmark in the Patterson community of upper Happy Valley.

The Ferguson Post Office serves the Wilkes County part of lower Happy Valley. It is right beside the Ferguson Volunteer Fire Department.

Another landmark is the Patterson Fire Department in upper Happy Valley.

This is an old sign for the Patterson Fire Department outside the main station.

The middle part of Happy Valley is served by the Yadkin Valley Fire Department in Caldwell County.

The Ferguson Volunteer Fire Department in Wilkes County serves eastern or lower Happy Valley.

Blue Ridge Tissue

Blue Ridge Tissue is a successful business in Patterson in upper Happy Valley that one of my musician friends, Jon Doll, helps manage. There were other names of the mill before it was Blue Ridge Tissue. The first mill was called Doll Brothers Paper. It was sold by his grandfather, to Cellu-Products Company (paper), its second name. Thirdly it was Sealed Air (paper mill still). Fourthly it was Omni Supply (paper), and currently (fifth) it's Blue Ridge Tissue.

Above are two photos of the paper mill when it was called Cellu-Products. Photos provided by Jonathan Doll. Used with permission.

Happy Valley Medical Center

There's also the Happy Valley Medical Center that serves western Happy Valley and the whole Lenoir area They also have a satellite office, the Collettsville Medical Center, for folks who live in Collettsville, NC and further up the mountain towards Blowing Rock, NC. Those in the eastern part of Happy Valley are served by the **West Wilkes Medical Center** in Ferguson, NC.

Yadkin River Trail, aka the Greenway

I've enjoyed walking the beautiful trail for exercise. The combined asphalt and dirt trail extends for about 2 miles. My favorite part, the lower Greenway begins near the Hill Billy Trading Post (near the intersection of Hwy. 268 and the Yadkin River Road). This book's cover picture shows you the beginning of this part of the Greenway.

The trail eventually ends at a flag pole with a little park surrounding it. Then you turn around and follow the Greenway back to the parking lot. The river to one side and woods on the other side makes for a nice pastoral experience and good exercise as well.

The upper part of the Greenway begins at the Happy Valley Ruritan Club on the Yadkin River Road near the Happy Valley Elementary School and ends at the bridge at the intersection of Hwy. 268 and the Yadkin River Road. You either cross Hwy. 268 to continue walking the lower section, or retrace your steps to the Ruritan Club parking lot.

Hill Billy Trading Post

Here are two of four Hill Billy Trading Post Signs at the store If you see these signs, you are near the Greenway entrance. This is a quaint little store featuring a variety of collectibles and cold drinks for thirsty passersby who have just enjoyed the Yadkin River Trail. If you visit the Greenway, don't forget to drop by there when they're open, for they also have local crafts and sometimes rare toys.

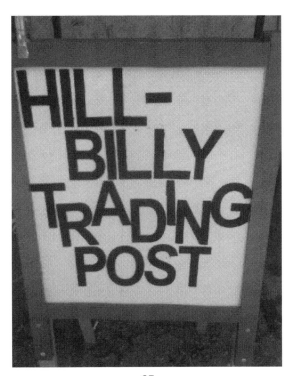

Cheeks Crossroads

There are two main stores in west Happy Valley and the area around it. One is the Yadkin Valley Grocery on Hwy. 268 and the other is Cheeks Convenience & Grill, which we call locally "Cheeks Crossroads." Cheeks is located on Blowing Rock Blvd. (Hwy 321) just north of Lenoir. The store has a large gas station and convenience area with Cheeks' Grill restaurant inside. It is a popular local stopping place with good ratings on food and service.

MUSEUMS

Interest in the historic and cultural opportunities is important in the region around both upper and lower Historic Happy Valley.

Caldwell Historical Museum

The local museum in Caldwell County is the Caldwell Historical Museum in Lenoir, NC. You can visit the museum and find out more about the area and its history.

Caldwell Historical Museum is located near historic Downtown Lenoir at 112 Vaiden St. SW. Tours are available. Admission is free, but donations are always welcome.

Wilkes Heritage Museum

The local museum in Wilkes County is the Wilkes Heritage Museum in Wilkesboro, NC. The Museum used to be the Wilkes County Courthouse. Tom Dooley, aka Tom C. Dula, was originally brought to trial for the murder of Laura Foster there, but the proceedings were eventually moved to Statesville in Iredell County, where he was convicted and hung on May 1, 1868. The museum is quite extensive and well worth the price of admission. They also have a great gift shop.

Whippoorwill Academy and Village

Whippoorwill Academy and Village is located in Ferguson, NC. It consists of a collection of old buildings that have been restored and moved to the property for historical and educational purposes. The structures include a Daniel Boone replica cabin, a blacksmith shop and a church.

The Whippoorwill Academy building itself was the original old school house in Ferguson. Also on the grounds is a museum dedicated to the Tom Dooley legend. It has paintings, photographs and accounts of what past Dula descendants believe happened. There are many opportunities to learn about the history of the area and enjoy cultural activities throughout the summer months.

Happy Valley Elementary School

Years ago. the Happy Valley Elementary School used to be just Happy Valley School which educated students from the first grade through high school. Dr. Gerald M. Bolick was principal of Happy Valley School for many years. He can still be seen working on his property with a big red tractor. He's always ready to impart some of the history of the area to curious passersby.

Dula-Hulme Cemeteries

There are two Dula-Hulme cemeteries in Happy Valley. On the east end (or Lower Happy Valley) is the Dula Hill location. That is where the original settler, William Dula, and his wife homesteaded. They and many of their offspring are buried there. According to Beth Hickman Hage, her 4th great grandfather, William Dula, and William Lenoir owned most of Happy Valley between them at one time. Of note, William Dula's brother, Bennett, was Tom Dooley's grandfather. Their side of the family were considered "ridge runners" (mountain farmers) and were not well-to-do.

On the west (upper) end of Happy Valley is the Chestnut Hill cemetery. The property is now owned by Dr. Bolick who was previously mentioned. His antebellum home, Chestnut Hill, is picture above. "Antebellum" means the house was built before the Civil War. The cemetery is up above the house.

The Chestnut Hill property was adjoined by the Redcliff property owned by William Dula's grandson, Alfred. He and his wife, Evelyn Corpening Dula, had six children. Mrs. Dula passed away and Alfred took to wife (not legally) Harriet Harshaw, a slave of mixed parentage. They had eight children together.

Today black and white cousins, descendants of Alfred Dula, come together for family reunions and other activities. It is a testament to the love and inclusivity of Family, which just happens to have sprung from Happy Valley.

Caldwell Arts Council

The Caldwell Arts Council is located at 601 College Avenue SW in Lenoir, NC. The building houses the Caldwell Arts Council Gallery. There are many programs offered at the Arts Council including Caldwell Junior Appalachian Musicians, which I will elaborate on in the music section.

Cultural Arts Council of Wilkes

The Cultural Arts Council of Wilkes is located at 913 C St. in North Wilkesboro. The building houses the Wilkes Art Gallery. The Arts Council has programs promoting the arts in Wilkes County.

Historic Happy Valley Mile Markers

According to the Caldwell Arts Council website, in their "Our History" section, in 2005 they began their "Historic Happy Valley Project." This was the result of receiving a grant from the North Carolina Arts Council. They basically hired local historians and folklorists to research the history of Happy Valley. The project was completed in 2008 with the installation of 24 Historic Happy Valley mile markers along Hwy. 268 from Caldwell County to Wilkes County.

Historic Happy Valley may extend a little before and beyond them. Notice that the floral embellishment for each mile marker differs from one to the other. I estimate that all told, the area that locals call Happy Valley runs from west to east (or upper to lower) about 28 miles.

I hope this book will help convey to you that here's lots to see in Happy Valley. Historic Happy Valley mile marker #3 is near the Patterson School, now called the Patterson Science Center. Mile marker #9 is near Laura Foster's grave site and near the area for the Happy Valley Fiddlers Convention. Mile marker #15 is near Tom Dooley's grave site. Mile marker #24 is about a half mile west of Reservoir Road which crosses over Kerr Scott Dam, which I feel marks the end of Historic Happy Valley.

Please note that markers #8, #11, #14, #16, and #21 appear to be missing so do not wreck trying to find them. Below are some examples of the mile markers with the various floral decorations on them.

Enjoy driving on scenic Hwy 268 which winds through the Valley and take in the history you pass along the way.

CHAPTER 5
Music

Pickin' and Grinnin'

Things change, attesting to accents, lilts, timbre... things like that.

Why do people's accents develop a particular way in a particular region? Perhaps, in part, the same way that the Celtic music sound drifted more towards the Bluegrass sound in the Appalachians. It is because of topography, for example, where it's hard to share and get to other places because of the mountainous landscape itself (especially in times when cars weren't around or common). Above is a beautiful view of Happy Valley east to west looking from Mountain View Overlook at W. Kerr Scott Reservoir. Notice Grandfather Mountain in the background.

The shape of the sounds can change both in language and in music because of this isolation. People's memories aren't perfect. People's memories of music that was brought into their home, for example, deep in a Valley somewhere, may not always be accurate. So, differences can develop because of this and happy accidents can also occur this way (like the development of Bluegrass).

Particular stylings in music can get added and/or left out. Melodies can vary. Even lyrics can be adapted and changed from person to person.

Nowhere is this more obvious than in the famous song titled "Tom Dooley" (occasionally called the "Ballad of Tom Dooley").

Tom Dooley

Artistic conception of Tom Dooley in a North Carolina Infantry private's uniform in the Confederate army. Tom's facial features are based on photos said to be his older brother and his mother (found in the Tom Dooley Museum on the Whippoorwill Academy and Village campus) and a description from a local newspaper dated May 2, 1868. Tom was not handsome, but could be called good-looking. (Brown, F. C., p. 705) Art by Leila McMichael. Used with permission.

Traditional tunes like "Tom Dooley" and "Brown Mountain Lights" are very popular here especially since their story origins are local and semi-local.

"'Tom Dooley' fits within the wider genre of Appalachian 'sweetheart murder ballads.' A local poet named Thomas Land wrote a song about the tragedy, titled 'Tom Dooley' (which was how Dula's name was pronounced), shortly after Dula was hanged. In the documentary *Appalachian Journey* (1991), folklorist Alan Lomax inaccurately describes Frank Proffitt as the 'original source' for the song. There are several earlier known recordings, notably one that Grayson and Whitter made in 1929, approximately 10 years before Proffitt cut his own recording." ("Tom Dooley (song)," 2019)

The above quote touches on the problem with the song "Tom Dooley" and its disputed origin and subsequent variations.

A very interesting read on the story of Tom Dooley and Laura Foster is found in the online version of Dr. Frank C. Brown's *North Carolina Folklore*, Volume II (Full text of "The Frank C. Brown Collection of North Carolina Folklore; the folklore of North Carolina, collected by Dr. Frank C. Brown during the years 1912 to 1943, in collaboration with the North Carolina Folklore Society"), courtesy of Internet Archive, a non-profit organization dedicated to providing access to knowledge. The link is found in the reference section and if you want to know more than you ever wanted to know about the trial of Tom C. Dula and the three folk ballads it spawned, this is the best place to go. Just open the link and search for "Tom Dula and Laura Foster."

The online document contains the original 21-stanza poem "The Murder of Laura Foster" written by Thomas Land, a former captain in the Confederate Army relocated from Tennessee to the area and who was, in fact, a neighbor of the Fosters. Of interest to me is that Dr. Brown records a conversation with a Lenoir native, the late Mrs. Maude Minish Sutton, that reveals, among other things, a Happy Valley connection to the song.

> Mrs. Sutton in the second of two long notes, wrote "It was very popular in the hills of Wilkes, Alexander, and Caldwell counties in 1867. Many mountain ballad singers still sing it." After briefly noting the fact on which the ballad was based, she continued: "Last week I went out in Yadkin Valley section of Caldwell to see if I could get all the words to the song. . . . The ballad of Laura Foster and Tom Dula I collected from 'Red-Headed Calvie Triplett,' who lived in Lenoir a few years ago. I collected another version from Mrs. R. T. Lenoir, who got it from a servant on her plantation, Fort Defiance, in Caldwell county....
>
> Mrs. Sutton describes 'Tom Dula' as "a banjo tune" and says that it "was composed by an old Negro named Charlie Davenport...." (Brown, F. C., pp. 711-712)

If Mrs. Sutton's written testimony is correct, the lyrics to the song "Tom Dooley" were written by Charlie Davenport, a local African American banjo player (with the melody based on another song of that era first documented in 1851 per a *Wikipedia* article). Additionally, Dr. Brown's documentation alludes to the 19th century origins of the song by the following quote:

'Tom Dooley.' With music. From Thomas Smith, Zionville, Watauga county. Note by Dr. Brown: "Sung by Mrs. R. A. Robinson, Silverstone, N. C, 6/22/21." Mr. Smith says that the "verses are from a song which has been sung and played for many years (probably for over forty) in Watauga. . . . There is hardly a fiddler or banjo picker in our county who cannot play 'Tom Dooley.' " (Brown, F.C., p. 712)

Forty years from 1921 would give you the year of 1881, a mere 13 years after Tom Dula's hanging on May 1, 1868. As I said earlier, people's memories aren't perfect and the passage of time has no doubt caused people to change the words to songs, whether deliberately or not. But Dr. Brown's work does support the early origins of the song.

The earliest commercial recording of "Tom Dooley" was done in 1929 by G. B. Grayson and Henry Whitter. Unaware of this fact while hunting for mountain folk songs, Anne and Frank Warner met Frank Proffitt in Watauga County, and he sang and played "Tom Dooley" for them. Proffitt claimed a personal connection to the story; his grandmother lived in Wilkes County and knew both Tom Dula and Laura Foster he claimed. One source also said Frank Proffit claimed his grandmother wrote the song after hearing Tom Dula singing it on his coffin on his way to be hanged. ("The Story of Tom Dooley." 2019). In 1940, the Warners recorded and transcribed the written lyrics of "Tom Dooley" from Frank Proffitt officially.

Frank Warner, a musician in his own right, modified Frank Proffitt's version and released his own commercial rendition of "Tom Dooley" in 1952. After that the song was covered by many artists. When the Kingston Trio recorded it around 1958, thinking it was public domain. They had no idea they were going to be slapped with a lawsuit by representatives of Frank Proffitt and Frank Warner in a few short years. It was settled out of court. Though the legal hassle was inconvenient, the Kingston Trio put the song "Tom Dooley" on the map forever.

Unfortunately, the back story to the murder of Laura Foster is much more sordid than the lyrics of the song "Tom Dooley" would let on. You will have to refer to the link in the reference section "The Scary Truth: The Legend of Tom Dooley" on the North Carolina Ghosts website for that information.

Another Tom Dooley book called *Lift Up Your Head, Tom Dooley: The True Story of the Appalachian Murder That Inspired One of America's Most*

Popular Ballads was written by John Foster West, the brother of one of my father's earliest law partners, Ted West.

Another interesting side note, since we are in the music section, is that apparently Tom Dooley was a musician and is listed as such in a surviving muster role as a musician and a drummer (April 19, 2019, Wikipedia Contributors). Folklore has it he was also a fiddle player and some say a banjo player.

Brown Mountain Lights

Another popular ballad about a semi-local paranormal phenomenon is "Brown Mountain Lights" written by Scott Wiseman. I have enjoyed performing this song a lot (sometimes I sing "moon" instead of "stars" and a few other changes, but I follow it pretty closely). It's a relatively easy song for guitarists to play, in my opinion. Legends of the Brown Mountain Lights vary from Indian women searching for their fallen men after a great war to a faithful slave searching for his lost master, as an explanation of the lights. Most scientists think the Brown Mountain lights are a form of ball lightning or swamp gas. But no one knows for sure. The internet is full of pictures of the lights and even videos. I have not personally seen the Brown Mountain lights.

Here is a painting by Leila McMichael representing that legend. (1969. Used with permission.)

A popular Charlotte morning television program, *The Arthur Smith Show*, featured musician/singer Tommy Faile who was apparently the first musician to record "Brown Mountain Lights." He made the song very popular both locally and elsewhere. His beautiful bass rendition of the song can be found on Youtube. Of note, Arthur Smith, a talented musician and songwriter in his own right, wrote "Feudin' Banjos" in 1955 which was revived as "Dueling Banjos" and used in the film, *Deliverance*. The *Arthur Smith Show* ran for 32 years and was syndicated nationally.

When I'm playing with our family band, **Swims With Mink** (which includes me and my two older brothers) they always want me to perform "Brown Mountain Lights" or start our performance off with me doing it. These family reunion performances are almost always non-local because we like to gather in different areas, such as in Montana, Maine, Virginia and North Carolina with family.

Also pertaining to music are the proverbial "field hollers" which used to be more of an African American tradition often done during older times. It helped workers keep in rhythm while on the job, plus adding a little spirit. I remember working around my friend Sharon Dayton's house on the Cheeks Crossroads store side of the Valley (close to Setzer's Creek Rd.) and she would suggest that I sing while I worked there outside. That seemed to help me. I remember one song I would sing while working for her, "The Wind That Shakes the Barley." So, I can honestly say I've kind of done field hollers working in the Valley some time ago. Sharon helped to improve some of my visual art skills by working with me one on one. I wish she was still with us.

———————————

Although historically known for its Old Time (a genre of North American Folk music) and Bluegrass music, Caldwell County is also known for its Blues traditions. This area has demonstrated literally every type of music throughout the years. Even Happy Valley has played host to them in one form or another.

These types include: Blues, Classical, Traditional, Bluegrass, Gospel, Country, Rebel Country, R & B, Old Time, Bluegrass, Rock, Southern Rock, Folk Rock, Punk Rock, Gothic, Celtic, Celtic Rock, Jazz, Experimental, Pagan, Native American and other world genres. Here are a few of the notables in the music business in Lenoir.

James C. Harper School of Performing Arts

This area prides itself for example on high standards of music education, especially because of the late Captain James Harper, who founded the Lenoir High School band. Captain Harper was a big John Philip Sousa devotee. Sousa was an American composer and conductor known for his rousing military march music. He also created the Sousaphone, an instrument similar to a tuba, but designed for marching because wraps around the body of the player making it easy to carry. A school devoted to music and the performing arts was founded in Lenoir and named after Captain Harper. For many years it has provided a high level of excellence in music training. So symphonic / classical music musical traditions have carved out a cornerstone here locally.

Ed Whitener, who I have already mentioned, was my very first band teacher. I learned to play the trumpet under his direction. The trumpet became a big love for me; playing it was like a breath of fresh air.

I also want to take a moment to mention the late Jim Graeber and his sister, Camilla Graeber, who I spoke with just recently. They were both band directors of mine at Hibriten High School and were very influential on me. The band did a Mozart medley my first year of high school. It was my favorite music moment up to that point and one of my favorite moments still today. Jim let me try to direct that very piece one time when we were rehearsing it. He may have had to go handle something. The medley was designed from the screenplay *Amadeus*, so I was already very familiar with the music.

It was during my further band participation that I still have one of my fondest memories. We performed "Night on Bald Mountain" a symphonic poem by Russian composer Modest Mussogorsky. A symphonic poem is a single orchestral movement that evokes the telling of a story or a poem. We played it while we marched on the football field one cold October night at Hibriten. You could not have asked for a more perfect setting for such an iconic, dark piece. I fell in love with "Night on Bald Mountain" as a child because of its inclusion in the Disney movie *Fantasia*.

John Craig was my last band teacher when I finished high school at West Caldwell. One of John Craig's current projects is directing the Silvio Martinat Swing band.

I feel very lucky to have been in two different marching bands in my life.

Marvin's One Stop

A cornerstone in the local music shop business is Marvin's One Stop record shop. It is one of the oldest, still operating businesses in historic Downtown Lenoir, and Marvin Gilreath, 78, still runs it. Even my older brother remembers Marvin from his Lenoir Junior High School days. I've known him since 1999 or thereabouts. But when I later worked at the Supreme restaurant, I often used to take my breaks in Marvin's store. He has some of the broadest range of vinyl records I've ever seen. Marvin and his record store was featured in the *Hickory Daily Record* on April 21, 2013.

Dead Wax Records

Chris Crookston runs Dead Wax Records. He is a musician in different area bands and always helps support local artists sometimes by putting on shows on the record store property just as Joe Young did sometimes at his store. I enjoyed going to some of these shows; it was always a punk rock potpourri. Chris is currently in a band called Thing Sloth.

Along with businesses and organizations that promote music and music awareness, we must salute and recognize individual performers in our area. To paraphrase Lydia Loveless, if you say you support the music and don't support the artists, like what's the point? In this section, I would like to highlight some of our famous local artists (international and regional), and/or those with a local connection, starting with those who have passed.

Famous Musicians with Caldwell County Connection

Doc Watson

The late great Arthel Lane "Doc" Watson from Deep Gap, NC, played often in Lenoir during the 1940's and 50's. Doc is considered one of the best in his music genre (Folk and mountain ballads, with strong roots in Country and early Bluegrass) with an unprecedented flat-picking style. Greg Watson, a Lenoir native currently living in Delaware with his wife, Teresa, relates that

his uncle, R. G. Watson, had a live radio program out of Lenoir on WJRI. Greg's father, Jesse, and other uncle, Hartzel, along with R. G., would come and play in the storefront of O. P. Lutz's Furniture Company (built in 1939, commonly known locally as the old Roses building, now a historic landmark).

Someone would bring Doc Watson down from Deep Gap and he would play with them on R. G's program. It was during this timeframe, and in Lenoir, that Doc received his nickname in honor of Sherlock Holmes' famous sidekick. According to Dan Miller, Editor and Publisher of *Flatpicking Guitar Magazine*:

"Doc acquired his nickname when he was eighteen years old. He was playing with his friend Paul Greer at a remote control radio show being broadcast from a furniture store in Lenoir. The radio announcer decided that 'Arthel' was too long a name to announce on the radio and suggested they think of another name to call him. A young woman in the audience yelled out, 'Call him 'Doc.' The name stuck and has been with him ever since."

("A Biography of Doc Watson." page 5]

The group also played at Hogwaller. Greg said back then Hogwaller was a hub of musical activity for the locals and local musicians. It was located in a small building down in "the holler" below the General Electric store on a street that ran between General Electric and Smithey's Department store. You could get food and drink down there and listen to musicians play. From there, musicians could walk into the bottom part of the furniture building, climb upstairs into the first floor of the store and easily go sit in the window front of the O. P. Lutz Furniture store and perform for R. G.'s program and others. The post office was across the street and people would come get their mail, then cross the street and watch the musicians play during their live broadcasts.

Years later, Greg got to play informally with Doc Watson at the Old Rock School. They did "Sleep Baby Sleep" which was originally cut in 1927 by Jimmie Rodgers, who is considered the father of country music and was one of Doc's favorite musicians. Later Greg asked him how they were related, and Doc said, "I definitely know we are kin; I just can't tell you how." One of Greg's fondest memories is hanging with Doc at MerleFest. MerleFest was began by Doc to honor his late son Merle Eddy Watson, who was killed in a tractor accident. MerleFest meets in the spring in Wilkesboro, NC. It attracts local musicians from the Valley and all over the world.

An interesting fact about Doc Watson was that although he was blind, he could fix watches. A close relative of his that I knew told me that he would come in and see him with watch parts just scattered everywhere and Doc could put all of those parts back together and fix watches. Remarkable!

Carl Story

The late great Carl Story was born in Lenoir, NC. Carl was a very influential bluegrass musician and singer. He was dubbed the father of Bluegrass Gospel music by the governor of Oklahoma. Story's band was the "Rambling Mountaineers" and he himself played with a lot of famous country music personages over his career. Local Gospel musicians Greg Watson and his wife, Teresa, were instrumental in getting a section of Hwy 18 in Lenoir (in the Gamewell community) named the "Carl Story Sr. Memorial Highway."

Pop Ferguson

Another famous Lenoir artist is the late Clyde "Pop" Ferguson, Sr. I went to several of his concerts while he was alive and have his autograph. I also know his son, Clyde, Jr. Pop was such an influential blues musician, but he was also an educator. Pop Ferguson and the Blues Review frequently performed for diverse audiences statewide, showcasing historical songs from the 1920's - 1950's. In 2008, "Pop" was inducted into the Folkways Museum of the Smithsonian Institution and the Library of Congress' National Recording Registry for his work in African-American music. Clyde Jr. continues his father's legacy of educating through music.

That brings us to a discussion of **Piedmont Blues**. Pop Ferguson exemplified Piedmont Blues. Piedmont Blues is a guitar style, specific to fingering, combining a rhythmic bass pattern with a syncopated treble pattern. The resulting combination has been compared to ragtime rhythms.

Piedmont Blues differs from other styles by its ragtime-based rhythms. One of the earlier recording artists included Blind Boy Fuller who was instrumental in influencing Pop Ferguson, whose first performance attempt was Fuller's "Step It Up and Go" at a tent revival. His father, a Holiness preacher, stopped him and sent him home.

"Recording artists such as Blind Blake, Josh White, Buddy Moss, and Blind Boy Fuller helped spread the style.... Blind Boy Fuller's 1940 recording of "Step It Up and Go" sold over half a million copies." ("Piedmont Blues," 2018)

No discussion of Piedmont Blues is complete without mentioning the late **Etta Baker** from Caldwell County. She was a very famous blues singer and musician. She and Pop Ferguson knew each other. Today there are many Piedmont Blues concerts across the South, honoring and carrying on this great blues tradition. In our area, the Harris Brothers carry on this tradition in their music.

The following music information is more specific to upper Happy Valley area which I am most familiar with, having played with or attended performances of many of these artists and groups. I am very sure there are many talented musicians in lower Happy Valley and I mean no disrespect for not mentioning them here. I salute them instead and regret that I do not know them to mention them, but hope to meet many in the future!

Local Mainstream Musicians

Richard Pinson

My friend, Richard Pinson, is a fine example of a local Classical concert pianist who is also well versed in contemporary music. He studied at the Julliard School of Music. I have seen him perform a lot in the area. He is well known for his expertise in performing Rachmaninoff pieces and many other great historical composers.

Bob Kogut

Bob Kogut is a very talented local fiddle player who appears in many music venues in and around Caldwell County. Bob is well known for his beautiful handcrafted fiddles that he sells worldwide.

Bob Henson

Bob Henson is an excellent local musician and songwriter. He serves as an Interim Program Director for the Caldwell Arts Council, and as such works heavily with the Caldwell County Junior Appalachian Musician program. He helped popularize Guy Clark's song, "Homegrown Tomatoes." Bob's wife, Debbie, was my high school Early American History teacher.

Local Musical Groups

Strictly Clean and Decent

Strictly Clean and Decent is a popular acoustic trio that plays a lot of different music styles including Bluegrass, folk, Celtic, and classic country. They perform at a lot of events and even travel to Ireland to perform. The trio consists of Patrick and Kay Crouch and Ron Shuffler.

Puddingstone

Formed first as a trio, Puddingstone now has 6-7 members, among whom are Denise Baxter-Yoder, Mike Willis and David Abernethy, as I recall. Puddingstone offers a variety of musical styles, including Americana, Celtic,

Folk, New Age, and Renaissance. I've known Denise since I was in the 4th grade.

Silvio Martinat Swing Band

The Silvio Martinat Swing Band -- named for founding member, band leader, and trumpet player Silvio Martinat -- was formed in 1988 as a performance class at CCC&TI. Since 2012 John Craig has served as band leader. I sat in on trumpet with them years ago. The band has been performing for 31 years and features Big Band Swing music popular in the 30's and 40's, but also performs some 50's and 60's music.

Happy Valley Fiddler's Convention

Though not technically a group, this is a specifically Happy Valley musical event that happens annually over the Labor Day weekend, bringing fiddlers and other musicians to gather at 3590 NC-268 (near where Laura Foster is buried) to play and sing and enjoy all kinds of mountain music and culture. Fridays are generally free, but there is a fee for Saturday and Sunday. For more information, go to www.happyvalleyfiddlers.org.

MerleFest

Annually held in Wilkesboro in April, MerleFest was founded by Doc Watson to honor his son, Merle, who was tragically killed in a farming accident. The festival is a fundraiser for Wilkes Community College and brings together musicians from all genres to play, resulting in what has been termed a mix of "Traditional Plus."

Other Festivals

A couple of other festivals near Happy Valley that offer mountain music and celebrate Appalachian culture are the North Carolina Blackberry Festival in Caldwell County in July and the Brushy Mountain Apple Festival in Wilkes County in October.

Alternative / Underground Music

Joe Young

The late Joe Young was the founding guitar player for the world reknown band Antiseen, which originated locally and has been around since the very early days of punk rock music.

"Antiseen became notorious and sometimes controversial voice in Southern punk rock." ["Antiseen Guitarist Dies of Heart Attack. *Charlotte Observer*, May 5, 2014]

Joe grew up in Lenoir. He and his brother, Jeff, ran the Repo Depot, one of Lenoir's iconic record stores for 10 years, and as such supported many local fledgling bands and music groups. His support for young area artists helped establish and inspire individuals, and the local bands associated with them, like Jon Doll, Chris Crookston, Chris Church, Chris Berry, Dave Whisnant and myself, just to name a few.

He is still remembered fondly, especially locally. I think it is mostly because of Joe that alternative / underground music has been a continuing part of the local music circuit today.

Jon Doll

One of our local Happy Valley musicians is Jon Doll (sometimes known as Johnny Dollface). He is a guitarist, singer/songwriter. He is one of my best friends. He and I have played together numerous times. One of the songs he wrote about Happy Valley is "The Valley Forever" He's been in several bands such as 5 Gallon Bucket, Happy Valley Social Club, Space Rocket and Legions (the one that I fronted). I first heard about him online where he went by the name of "Some Local Loser" where he invited me to play at the first "Flatwood Stock."

The rest is history. Nowadays I call him "Some Local Lewis," not to use excessive coded language or inside jokes in this book. We are both fans of Stephen Kings' "Pet Sematary."

A few lines of his song, "The Valley Forever," are:

As the air gets thinner you start to see the day unfold
If heaven is real it looks like those mountains and hills
and we'll be waiting in the Valley below

He also wrote a song called "12 Hour Shift," which is a very popular song he performs throughout the Valley and in town.

Dave Whisnant

Dave is my friend who I first met at William Lenoir Middle School and I've known him intermittently ever since. He is a local Happy Valley singer/bass player who has been in many working bands. LSC is one of the bands Dave is most noted to have participated in. He's also an expert rock climber to this day. You haven't seen anything until you have seen him perform live.

Chris Berry

I have been friends with Chris since my early days of Hibriten High School. He's another popular, experienced bass player from the Lenoir area. There were a lot of "firsts" I experienced growing up around him. Needless to say, some of these were very humorous.

Chris Church

Another artist who has lived in the valley and really made some bounds in music is Chris Church. He has fronted bands like Dang and is active in several bands. Along with covers, he is a unique original singer/songwriter in his own right too. He has also lived in Happy Valley. He's one of the funniest people I've ever met.

Doug Davis

Doug Davis, a multi-instrumentalist who I have worked several musical projects with, is proficient in old-time traditional music as well as rock, alternative rock, and the like. He's also a talented art teacher.

Will Willis

Will Willis is a friend of mine, a great singer and guitarist, who has really taken off professionally. He was associated with some of the later Hogwaller programming in historic Downtown Lenoir.

Lyra Wakefield

Another very talented artist is Lyra Wakefield. She is a fine guitarist and singer, who has produced an EP/demo of mine called "Perpetual Vision Quest." She and I were also in a band called Alphabet Disorder and we played some at Catawba Valley Brewing company in Morganton. Lyra, one of my ex-wife's children, lives in NY now and is currently in a band called Waking Dream.

David Lovatto

David is a local seasoned singer / guitarist who has played with most local artists around here, along with Muddy Waters and Jimi Hendrix. He and I have played some events and he has been influential in helping me get gigs where we performed together. He has got a tremendous repertoire and, if you're not careful, yours will increase if you play with him.

Sam Edmisten

Sam Edmisten is also from Happy Valley. Both of his parents and most of his relatives are from there. He lived on the Hollywood Ridge Road up on Miller Hill overlooking the Optimist baseball park, next door to his grandparents and great grandparents for several years. Sam is a talented guitar player and singer, and has a marvelous stage presence.

J. P. (Jon Parsons)

J. P. is a talented singer, guitarist and songwriter. The earliest song I heard him perform, and he also wrote, was "Hey Baby, If You Ever Wanna Rock 'n' Roll." This was in Chris Berry's old basement and later I saw him perform it on stage at Hibriten High School. It's stuck in my head ever since because to me it's a catchy song. He sang and performed it on electric guitar. J. P. can also play the bouzouki, originally a Greek stringed instrument.

Jeff Livingston

Jeff and I go back pretty far, and I remember many a crazy night at my old apartment at Cross Creek. We wrote a song together there, circa 1990 called "Gunned Down In The Sand." The song was performed as late as 2011 by one of my music projects, Legions.

Other notable musicians that are local, many of whom I've been blessed to play with, are: Brian Beaver, Brad Edwards (who lives in the Valley), Grayson Crump ("Cap'n Crump"), and Richard Van Stavern ("Rated R" J. R.).

Some of the gentlemen I have mentioned above have overlapped with each other in playing within different bands. All of these individuals have been influential in the music scene always demonstrating how to keep it real. Or as Johnny Dollface likes to say, "the Rrrrreal!"

Basically, it seems one out of about five people play guitar in this greater Caldwell County area. This may sound excessive, but I don't think this is too much of an exaggeration.

There are many other musician friends that are dear to me that I have left out for time and space constraints, but they have also made a tremendous mark in the local music community. You know who you are.

Below is a picture of a CD titled "Historic Happy Valley: A North Carolina Cultural Experience" offered by the Caldwell Arts Council in Lenoir, NC, in conjunction with the installation of the Historic Happy Valley mile markers. It contains interviews from residents of Happy Valley from all walks of life, historic information, cultural heritage, and a lot of musical tradition. One of the more interesting sections had the late Pop Ferguson, who was mentioned earlier, stating that he played quite often in the Valley.

I am grateful for the gift of this CD. As of this writing, I'm not sure of the current availability of the CD, but you can contact the Caldwell Arts Council to ask.

A Word on the Visual Arts in the Happy Valley Area

Many musicians are also visual artists as well. I myself am one of these people. I have mostly concentrated on musicians in my book because I consider myself a musician first and foremost.

Below is a monochromatic acrylic painting I did of a mountain scene inspired by Happy Valley and our local mountain area.

"Late Winter." Acrylic by JHG 2017

There are many good art programs in Caldwell County, both in the school system and through organizations such as the Women's Club which features art contests for various ages. The Caldwell Arts Council is home to a fine art gallery and has a gift shop where local artisans can sell their wares. The Wilkes Art Gallery also features exhibits of local artists, classes and a gift shop.

Several local Caldwell County artists that I know personally, like Charlie Frye and Andrew Atkin, have studios in Lenoir. Always try to patronize your own local artists and crafts persons, as well as musicians.

Jon Parsons, a friend of mine from West Caldwell High School -- not to be confused with another friend Jon Parsons ("J.P.") a friend of mine from Hibriten High School -- is a young aspiring visual artist. Jon has taken advantage of some of the Caldwell Arts Council's art programs and his painting has improved dramatically.

There are many venues for all kinds of arts and crafts including shows, festivals and conventions, both in Happy Valley and in other areas. To find out where and when these events occur, contact the arts council closest to you.

CHAPTER 6
Natural History

I would like to dedicate this section to Bob Holland,
a friend who has tremendous knowledge about Natural History.

Happy Valley is a rich location for all kinds of wildlife. It is located in part of the Yadkin/ Pee Dee River Basin and is surrounded by beautiful forests and meadows teeming with birds, insects, fish, reptiles and amphibians.

THE TWIN POPLARS

The Twin Poplars is on the other side of Highway 321 located somewhere near the Warrior Road which could be considered part of the Valley.

The Twin Poplars are a product of a Catawba and a Cherokee Indian peace treaty in 1737. After a very long and fierce week-long battle at Warriors Gap over the Catawba's friendly association with the white man and the Cherokees anger over that fact, they arrived at a truce. They erected a small mound of stones and they tied the two trees together symbolizing the peace treaty.

The tree is still seen today and is used as a popular Geocaching landmark. According to some, the legend of the Brown Mountain lights is tied into the war between the Catawba and Cherokee and Indian maidens searching for their dead and wounded.

LEGEND OF BIGFOOT

"If you saw Bigfoot [in the Valley], what would you say to em? Well, I'd say, 'Come on down, Sasquatch, let's take a good look at ye!' " (paraphrased) ["Bigfoot & Witches." Documentary. *Secrets of the Unknown* series. (c) 1987]

Valley 'Squatch or "Pattersquatch" (a phrase I have coined) have not been reported. But sightings have occurred in both Caldwell and Burke counties in years past. North Carolina is a prime Bigfoot-loving state, boasting sightings, museums and two festivals, one of which is in Marion, NC in September every year.

FISH

Jokes about Bigfoot in the Valley can lead to local discussions of cryptozoology. A form of cryptozoology could be the crossbreeding of local wild fish. I am not an expert on hybrid fish breedings, though catching a large "cut-bow" (a cross between a Cutthroat Trout and a Rainbow Trout) in Montana turned my curiosity more to hybrid fish. I found out that Atlantic Salmon can cross breed with Brown Trout successfully in the wild. Brown Trout and Brook Trout cross-breedings create the Tiger Trout. Warmouth (which already looks like a cross between a Bass and a Bluegill) can cross breed with Bluegill and Green Sunfish (which also has the body build of a

Warmouth). I have caught Warmouth in the Valley, but I have caught more Rock Bass than Warmouth there.

Some Sunfish apparently can crossbreed at will depending on environment. Bluegill, Redear, Pumpkinseed, and Green Sunfish can all produce offspring between themselves. According to "Hybrid Black Bass" by Steve Quinn, scientists artificially crossbred Largemouth Bass with Warmouth, Green Sunfish and Bluegill, but crossing Crappie and Rock Bass failed.

White Bass and Striped Bass can crossbreed in the wild but are sometimes bred in hatcheries to create a high energy game fish called a Hybrid Striped Bass or Whiterock Bass.

Warmouth, Smallmouth Bass and Rock Bass typically have red eyes. You have to be careful not to confuse them. Largemouth Bass can also occasionally have red eyes. If red-eye fish crossbreed with a species that doesn't have red eyes, would they create a red-eyed hybrid fish? According to Quinn, some researchers successfully crossed Largemouth Bass with Smallmouth Bass and the offspring was not sterile and continued to reproduce with both types. So, catching local red-eyed fish has heightened my attention to possible local hybridity and perhaps multi cross-breedings. You can still report caught fish to the local store in the Valley.

Some species of fish found in the Yadkin River that flows through Happy Valley:

• Largemouth Bass -- usually no red eyes, member of the Sunfish family
• Smallmouth Bass -- usually red eyes, member of the Sunfish family
• Red Eye Rock Bass -- usually light colored, but sometimes blackish. Has distinctive red eyes
• Horny Heads -- Hornyhead Chub, a type of commonly caught, blunt-headed species of fish of the Carp family. We've often called them "bait stealers!"
• Sucker Fish -- a couple different kinds, bottom feeders
• Carp -- Grass Carp are initially from China and have been sterilized; used to control vegetation in lakes and rivers; other Carp were introduced in the 1800's and are common in North America. I've actually caught a regular Carp in the Valley
• Trout – Several kinds (Brown Trout, Brook Trout (also known as Specks or Brookies), Rainbow Trout, are abundant in the Valley's Yadkin River until it starts to get fished out. Some people will take a 1/2 dozen trout back with

them in a day, which makes for difficult findings for other anglers. Trout rivers are usually restocked annually in April.

• <u>Bluegill</u> aka Brim or Bream -- member of the Sunfish family also sometimes called Pan Fish in certain area. Other similar Sunfish members are Redear, Pumpkinseed, Green Sunfish and Rock Bass

• <u>Crappie</u> -- White and Black Crappie are both native to NC and are members of the Sunfish family. White Crappie have blotches in broken vertical bars on their body, while Black Crappie have irregular dark blotches. I don't think I've ever caught a Crappie in the Valley.

• <u>Brown Catfish</u> and other species of Catfish -- Catfishing at night is fun in certain places. I remember catching mostly brown or brown-colored Catfish in the Valley. One day during a heavy rain and flood, I caught some whitish-colored Cats. This is an example of what you can catch in these kinds of conditions.

Red Eye Rock Bass, angler Jon Doll, September 25, 2018 8:30 am,
Buffalo Dam above Happy Valley.
All fish photos by Jon Doll and used with permission.

Close up of the eye of Red Eye Rock Bass.

Side view of Red Eye Rock Bass, above.

Regular Smallmouth Bass that angler Jon Doll caught in the Valley, right

A Hybrid Striped Bass that angler Jon Doll caught in Yadkin River in Happy Valley. "Sometimes they run up the river from Kerr Scott Lake to the Little Yadkin." Jon Doll says.

I was lucky, or blessed, to have a great place to fish in Happy Valley. For some reason, perhaps because it's the headwaters to the greater Yadkin, it seems that everything caught in the Happy Valley is a sport fish. A half of a night crawler on the bottom works well for catching most species in the Valley. Use a single or 2 ball shot (more or less 16 inches distance between bait and weight). Sometimes letting the worm dangle a little can help.

The VW rallies have been held on private land in the Valley. I have visited this area many times, and stayed there some, and that's one of the places I've enjoyed fishing in the past. I remember catfish were Sandra's favorite fish to catch. A lot of the land belonged to her family toward the east end of Happy Valley which was called River Run Ranch.

101

Here's another fish, a red eyed Smallmouth Bass caught by Jon Doll on April 19, 2019 11;19 am in the Yadkin River in Happy Valley. Photo by Jon Doll. Used with permission.

SNAKES

The difference between venomous snakes and non-poisonous snakes is the shape of the head and the pupils of the eyes. If a snake has a *distinctly* triangle-shaped head off of a narrow neck and slit pupils, it's poisonous. If a snake has more of a smooth head adjoining the neck and round pupils, it is nonpoisonous.

The Black Racer [aka Eastern Racer, also called Blue Racer] is a non-venomous snake. They are not protected in our state, but they are in Georgia]. Black Rat Snakes, or just Black Snakes as we commonly call them, are a different species. You can tell the difference between them because black Racers are black on their belly as well and much shinier than their Rat snake brethren. Black Snakes are not smooth and glossy; they have rough scales, have white on their bellies, and possibly whitish or greyish bands or markings on their upper body. The young are brown. Black Snakes are mostly found in the Piedmont and mountains while Racers are found in a much larger geographic range. Black Rat Snakes are more docile, and can make good pets, but Black Racers are more likely to strike at you and remain wild even in captivity.

[Eastern Kingsnake] File:Lampropeltis getula getula is licensed under CC BY 2.0

Some of the other common non-venomous snakes in the Valley are Kingsnakes, Garter Snakes, Corn Snakes and Eastern Worm Snakes. An example of a Kingsnake is pictured on the previous page. Bands of white can be more pronounced. Kingsnakes come in many different colors and patterns depending on geographical region.

My great grandfather Zach Lee Groome had a kingsnake in his corn crib and he threatened to "whup" anyone who messed with his snake because it protected the corn from rats and kept away other snakes. Kingsnakes are not poisonous and will help keep your property venomous snake-free.

Be very careful to know what our local VENOMOUS snakes look like if you are going out into the fields and woods. Be careful of Rattlesnakes (they come in all sizes) and Copperheads. The most common rattlesnake in our area is the Timber Rattlesnake. The Pygmy Rattlesnake is found throughout NC. The rattlesnake has a distinctive warning rattle if you get too close, though it is hard to hear a Pygmy's rattle.

Another reason to know exactly what a Copperhead looks like is because some non-venomous snakes have somewhat similar markings. To be safe, just move away from the area where you encounter any kind of snake. According to my best recollection, a friend of mine who is part Mi'kmaq (Micmac) Indian said they caught Tom Dooley up in Trade, TN near Copperhead Road. This might not be the best place to mention a fact about Tom Dooley, but we were discussing Copperheads and it reminded me.

Coral snakes are venomous, but do not live in our area. For any similarly banded snake, remember "Red on black, venom lack. Red on yellow, kill a fellow

A lot of people think the Water Moccasin or Cottonmouth Moccasin lives in our mountainous area of North Carolina, but they are incorrect. They have been mistaking the Black Racer and common nonvenomous water snakes (genus Nerodia) for Water Moccasins for years and killing them needlessly as a result. Black Racers have been known to kill other snakes.

Killing a NON-poisonous King Snake is like inviting poisonous snakes into your yard. They are immune to venom of poisonous snakes and will attack, kill and eat them. Black Rat Snakes, or just Black Snakes as we call them, eat tons of rats and mice and this is very beneficial. If a Black Rat Snake becomes annoying because it starts eating chicken eggs, try to capture and relocate it.

So Stop Killing Non-Poisonous Snakes! In fact, think twice before killing any wild animals on your property. Remember, it's their yard too. Always walk looking down where you are going while in the woods and meadows.

TURTLES, LIZARDS, AND AMPHIBIANS

We have several species of turtles and tortoises in Happy Valley. The difference between them is tortoises live on the land, while turtles live in the water some or all of the time. Happy Valley has Common Snapping Turtles, Eastern Box Turtles (the females have brown eyes and the males have red eyes), and some water turtles.

Lizards and amphibians that abound in the Valley are: Fence Lizards, Blue Tailed Skinks, Spring Lizards (really salamanders), Newts (found in still waters and have a flattened tail for swimming), various toads, frogs, and Bullfrogs. Additionally, in the rivers and branches can be found little black freshwater snails, crawdads (crayfish), minnows, and aquatic insect life.

MAMMALS

Black bear, bobcat, musk rat, weasel, beaver, ground hogs, badgers, otter, skunks, deer, bobcat, coyote (a kind of recent addition to our wildlife population), raccoon, opossum (don't kill opossums; they eat lots of ticks), squirrel, rabbits, rats, mice, voles and fox, to name a few. It's even said there may be a wolf or two in the mountains of North Carolina.

It appears that the Carolina panther (aka puma, cougar, mountain lion) may be extinct in our area, though reports persist. Years ago, while camping in the Valley, we heard a cry at night that sounded like a woman screaming. On another occasion, Sandra may have been chased by a large cat while she was driving a golf cart. She heard it roar and run through the leaves behind her. She did not turn around and drove away using as much power as the golf cart could muster.

The three most hunted animals by man, that I've noticed in the Valley, are deer, wild turkey and raccoon.

Our Friend, the Opossum

I want to talk a bit about the Opossum, commonly called "possum." It is the only marsupial in North America. They can look menacing, but they are not. In the wild, they eat lots of ticks and other insects. They are known to "play dead" when threatened. This involves falling over, opening their mouth, foaming or slobbering at the mouth (but they do not have rabies), and emitting a foul odor from their anal glands. Faking death will sometimes cause a prey animal to leave them alone and they can escape. Let's protect them.

"Opossum" by Cody Pope is licensed under Own Work (CC-BY-SA-2.5)

BIRDS

The Valley has a host of winged fowl, including songbirds like the Robin and Meadowlark; wrens, hummingbirds, cardinals, blue jays, owls, crows, doves, vultures, hawks, wild turkeys, eagles, kingfishers, woodpeckers, etc. Recent additions include pigeons and even gulls and other sea birds, in some cases, along with migratory Canada Geese and ducks.

One of my favorite moments while fishing in the Valley was watching two blackish-colored ducks with blue markings flying nearby.

INSECTS

No discussion of nature in the Valley is complete without mentioning the lowly insect. Some are beneficial, some are annoyances; and some can be harmful. All surely must have a purpose even if we cannot fathom it. They include: all manner of flies, butterflies, moths, honeybees, bumblebees, wasps, mosquitoes, stink bugs, fleas, ticks, spiders, ants, earthworms (good for bait!), caterpillars, beetles, hornets, etc.

The little sweat bee is the master of the sneak attack and they will make their presence known if rubbed the wrong way. Other stinging insects are wasps (including Yellow Jackets) and hornets, which can sting over and over. Honeybees, on the other hand, give their life when they sting.

Mosquitoes can carry viruses. Horse flies and wood flies also like blood. No stinging or biting insect is a fun experience, so be careful when you are in the great outdoors.

EDUCATE AND PROTECT

Bees & Honeybees: Save our Natural Pollinators

"Bee on a Dandelion" by Sandy, Bedfordshire is licensed under CC BY 2.0

The honeybee is our North Carolina state insect. Keep the bee in the Valley! Bees are in danger of dying out. Not only do they pollinate our plants, so food is produced, but they make honey for us to eat. Limit your use of pesticides in your lawns and gardens. Try to use environmentally friendly methods to control insects. Don't buy flowers and plants that are supposed to be "bee friendly," but are actually "bee killing" ones. These are plants and flowers that have been pre-treated with insecticides that kill bees!

Buy from the right sellers. Check before you buy. Even some major big-name businesses will sell pre-treated plants and flowers. Remember: "No Bees, No Food," so be careful what you buy. Also, there are several species of bees that live underground. Do not treat your grass with products that will kill them or their larvae. Do not step on honeybees in the yard. Watch where you walk! Also don't randomly kills wasps; many species hunt insect larvae that invades corn. You can coexist with wasps.

For more information, please check out the References section for an online link.

BEE Careful of the Plants and Flowers You Purchase!

Transplant some dandelions from your yard to a pot for the bees! It will help your yard and provide food for the bees. Dandelion leaves, especially when young and tender, and flowers are edible.

Invasive Species Note: Japanese Stilt Grass

My old friend, Bob Holland, a talented local naturalist advises everyone to pull Japanese Stilt Grass when you can because it chokes everything out and spreads rapidly. If not removed, or at least controlled, it ends up growing out of control choking out some native plants. Bob and I spent many hours at Laurel Cabin discussing nature, philosophy, and the like. For tips on getting rid of this invasive species, check out the references section for a good link online.

Invasive Species Note: Kudzu

Another invasive species from Japan that was brought in the early 20th century is Kudzu. That topic has been discussed many times in many ways in other places, so I won't belabor it here. Suffice to say, kill it when you can, but use environmentally friendly methods. Try to control it at the very least.

Note: Japanese Beetles, natural predator of Kudzu in Japan, were brought over after Kudzu ran rampant. They decided when they came to America, they liked roses better.

WILD FOODS

The forests and valleys are sources of many wild foods and herbs, some of which we have touched on elsewhere in the book (nuts, honey from honeybees, fish, persimmons, etc.), but there are other plants and roots that are edible as well.

Once of these is branch lettuce, found near natural springs, creeks and rivers alike. They are often served as "Kilt Lettuce" which involves using fresh leaves that have been "kilt" with hot bacon grease poured over them.

Another is Creecy (or creasy) greens is another seen at right. Creecy greens are a form of wild mustard. They appear early in the spring and have traditionally been eaten in the Appalachian Mountains. A lot of creecy grows in Happy Valley, along streams and in pastures.

You don't pull it up, you cut it off and leave the roots in the ground so as not to kill the plant. Harvest again next year. You have to harvest it before it blooms, because it becomes too bitter after blooming.

Watercress, a relative to Creecy, is found along branches and bogs and is good in salads and on sandwiches.

DISCLAIMER

You can do your own research on wild foods, but always exercise caution when eating something you're not sure of, especially mushrooms. It's best not to eat any mushrooms unless you're absolutely sure they won't make you sick.

CHAPTER 7

Real Good Recipes

*I would like to dedicate this section to the late Dorothy Greer,
who taught me how to can foods without a pressure canner
in the Valley.*

Fast as Lightnin' Pickled Peaches

12 fresh peeled ripe firm peaches, cut in halves
10 to 12 whole Cloves
3 or 4 Cinnamon sticks
 2 Vanilla beans, split up in strips and seeded (optional, can use 1 teaspoon
vanilla)
1 cup granulated Sugar
2 cups Apple Cider vinegar
Whole bottle of Honey
4 cups White wine
1/4 cup lemon juice
pinch of Salt
Sterile jars and lids enough to hold the peaches (you can do your own in
boiling hot water)

Directions

Prepare yer peaches by dippin' them in a hot water bath for about 10 seconds,
then toss them in an ice water bath to cool. This is best for peeling yer peach
skin off without losing the fruit, then cut them peaches in halves. Throw away
the pits. Split that vanilla bean in half and use the dull side of your knife to
scrape out the seeds. If you want to split the halves in smaller sections to
spread the flavor around, go ahead. If you want to wuse out, use vanilla
extract. I ain't lookin'. Put yer wine down! That's for the recipe!

Mix yer wine, vinegar, honey, sugar, cinnamon sticks and lemon juice in a
medium pot. Simmer and then cook for about 5 minutes. Add yer peaches and
cook until heated through, maybe about 6 minutes. Get your sterile jars and
using tongs or a spoon put yer peaches in the jars. Make sure your vanilla
bean pieces and cinnamon sticks are equal in all the jars. You may have to

break some cinnamon sticks up and cut up some pieces of bean. Pour the boiling syrup mix over the peaches, sticks and bean parts, and fill the jars right on up to about 1/4 inch below the rim of the jar. Seal the jars and let them cool. They will pop as they cool so you know you got yerself a good seal. These Fast as Ligtnin' Pickled Peaches will last in the fridge about a month.

Serve over roasted or fried chicken or anything else you think it would taste good with.

Provided by Sandra Renee Greer Groome

Beer Can Chicken (or Drunken Chicken)

Grill and charcoal
Whole, plucked and gutted young chicken carcass
1 can of imported Beer
1 can of domestic Beer
Salt to taste when served

Directions

Git yer grill fired up good en hot (allow coals to almost completely turn gray), cut the top of a beer can off carefully and insert it into your small, whole marinaded chicken. Put chicken sitting upright on the hot grill. Fill half the can with good imported beer. Top can off with a light domestic beer. Try to close the neck area up around the top of the chicken and can. Close lid gently. If the grill is not totally sealed because of the chicken sitting vertically on it, that's ok as long as there's about no more than few inches gap between the grill lid and the grill itself, vent slightly. Grill for about 2 to 2 1/2 hours (3 hours max).

Note: you may want to bast and/or marinate the chicken again some after it's on the grill. Charcoal recommended. Carefully remove chicken with can (making sure cooked beer doesn't wash the chicken) and enjoy the flavor! Most of the time, if done right, it's a "fall of the bone" experience! Save cut can for later use! Enjoy!

A variation on a basic recipe by James H. Groome

Marinade for Beer Can Chicken

Your marinade may be personal, but I also use a good store-bought or homemade, non-thick BBQ sauce, along with hot sauce or spicy dry rub.

Mighty Fine Coleslaw

If ya wanna make a real good Southern slaw, follow these here directions:

Take a good ole washed head o' cabbage and chop off as much as you'll need, leaving at least a lil' bit of green leaf for color. Chop it up real fine, to give it better taste and texture. This will also help the mayonnaise (some might use salad dressing) to stick to it way better. If yer not serving fish with it, add some finely diced (that means chop it up real fine) carrot for more color (also add a dash of salt). Add a little mayo at a time along with some sugar. Stir well and allow mixture to sit unrefrigerated for about 10 minutes. This way the sugar dissolves in your mix. You will see how thin or thick yer slaw is. Stir, then taste it to test yer sugar preference. Add more sugar and/or mayo as needed. Remember, ya'll, you (like in most recipes) can always add more, but you can't always take it away! Worst comes to worst, you can always add more cabbage if your slaw is too runny and/or if you have put in too much sugar. Add black pepper and stir (note: yinz might want to go heavy on the black pepper). Refrigerate, partially covered, and serve 20-30 minutes later. Enjoy!

A variation on "Southern Coleslaw" by James H. Groome

Red Eye Gravy Concept Recipe

2 pieces of country ham, sliced (about 6 ounces for you math inclined folks)
1/2 cup of strong black coffee
1/2 cup chicken broth or water (optional)
1/2 teaspoon of sugar
1 tablespoon of butter (unsalted if yer hoity-toity)

Directions
Pan fry yer country ham until you have browned both sides and have lots of driblets (drippings). Set yer ham off on a plate. Pour yer coffee in the pan and stir it up getting the ham driblets mixed in it. You can use straight coffee only or you can mix the chicken broth or water in as well. Add yer sugar. Cook it real quick like on medium heat until hot and well blended.

Serve on the ham or set it on the side. Also good on biscuits, potato cakes and grits (say it right, now y'all).

A variation on a basic recipe by James H. Groome

"One might think the 'red eye' name comes from the coffee (like a staying-awake reference) but it actually comes from the original way this gravy was prepared. In the first few recipes, the grease and coffee would interact with each other, causing what appeared to be a red human eye to form in the pan." (Chrisy, 9-27-18)

"The squirrels have taken back their recipe, so I have no recipe for squirrel gravy." JHG

Great Grandma Margie's Famous Oatmeal Raisin Cookies

3/4 cup vegetable shortening
1 cup firmly packed brown sugar
1/2 cup granulated sugar
1 egg
1/2 cup water
1 teaspoon vanilla
3 cups oats uncooked
1 cup all purpose flour
1 teaspoon salt (optional)
1/2 teaspoon baking soda
1/2 cup of raisins

Directions
Find ye an oven with a door. Preheat that there oven to 350 degrees. Combine all yer ingredients and divide it up into small cookie-sized balls and space them out on a greased baking sheet. Stick in the oven and bake 18-20 minutes or until golden brown. Remove from oven and cool before eatin'.

Handed down by Sandra Renee Greer Groome

NOTE; Margie Wakefield was Bill Wakefield's Grandmother, but my ex-wife called her "great" because she was a great grandma to their children. Margie lived at Table Rock, NC.

Grandma Johnson's Homemade Mayonnaise

2 1/2 cups sugar
5 eggs
1/2 cup of oil
2 tablespoon flour
2 tablespoon mustard
1/2 cup water
1/4 cup vinegar

Beat the eggs well. Add the 1/2 cup of oil to the beaten egg mixture and blend. Mix the 2 tablespoons of flour with the sugar and 2 tablespoons of mustard. Combine all ingredients. Beat well all together in a double boiler while cooking.

Provided by Kaeti Groome

Grandma Johnson's Corn Pudding

2 cans creamed corn
1/2 stick of butter
1 egg
2 tablespoons flour
1/4 cup sugar
1/4 cup milk or half & half

Mix all ingredients and put in greased casserole dish. Cook for 35-40 minutes at 350 degrees.

Provided by Kaeti Groome

Aunt Ona's Orange Salad

1 package of orange Jello
1 small cup water
1 pint of orange sherbet
1 can Mandarin oranges (drained)
1 can crushed pineapple
1 cup Cool Whip

Mix all together and cool. Serve chilled.

Provided by Kaeti Groome

Aunt Ona's Good Salad

1 package of lime Jello
1/3 cup water
1/2 cup fruit juice drained from pears

Boil all ingredients together for 7 minutes, pour into a bowl, then cool.

Add: 1 cup mashed pears
        1 cup marshmallows (small)
        1 cup cottage cheese

Mix all together and cool. Serve chilled.

Provided by Kaeti Groome

James' Venison Recipe

2-3 pounds venison steak medallions
2 cups finely diced onions
1 heaping tablespoon finely diced garlic
1 cup applesauce
2 tablespoons of apple-flavored whiskey (optional, but suggested)
1/2 cup sugar
1/2 teaspoon salt
1 1/2 teaspoons black pepper
1 teaspoon soy sauce
1 teaspoon of Worcestershire Sauce
1 tablespoon of extra virgin olive oil

Directions

Throw all the ingredients together in a bowl, mix together, and marinade yer medallions in it for about 2 hours in the ice box (refrigerator). It's best if left to marinade overnight. When ready to cook, remove yer medallions and allow to come to room temperature before cooking.

Place in a frying pan and pour that there marinade over and around them. Pan fry yer medallions and saute (pan frying while stirring) yer onions and garlic on medium temperature. Allow the meat to caramelize (that means turn they turn nice and brown) some, flipping the medallions occasionally and basting them with pan drippin's. Enjoy from the pan or throw on a grill for extra taste. You can also serve them on a plate by themselves or with other food.

"If it don't taste like beef after that, it missed a good chance!"

An original recipe from James H. Groome created in late winter 2019

Thanks

Thanks to all who contributed to this book including Leila McMichael for all her help with research and editing.

Thank you to the Dolls and the Greers: two families that I feel I have merged into, and who have helped allow me to enjoy the cradling benefits of this beautiful expanse called "the Valley."

Epilogue

Is Happy Valley Happy?

Being in beautiful places like the Valley can make one happy, but it's the people that inhabit or visit the place that have the most influence; if they're happy, then so is the Valley:

There are and have been many happy moments for a lot of us in Happy Valley, for certain. And that's what one should concentrate on as important; down to the joy of seeing yellow daffodils still blooming around dilapidated old houses or half buried along heavily wooded steep mountain sides around there. And I suppose if you see daffodils just randomly around in the forest with no sign of structures anywhere, then you can almost bet someone lived around there some time in the past and it was a place they called HOME.

And "that" makes you happy; to realize that there could have been a family in a now seemingly unsettled wilderness. Your imagination can almost take root and rise, as you yourself blend into the landscape as you explore it. And often times you can find very quiet places in the Valley, perfect for communing with nature. But always remember, wild animals like quiet places. Always be mindful you share the Valley with its wildlife. For me, it is the wildest of places that make me the happiest.

Help keep the Valley Happy: don't litter. This includes "micro trash" (small pieces of plastic and paper for example). It's easy to gather and throw away the big stuff, but the small micro trash is just as important. So, if you see any trash out in the Valley, or anywhere, please pick it up and discard it appropriately

I hope you enjoyed this book as much as I enjoyed researching, re-connecting with old friends because of it, and writing it. This is a labor of love that spans years! Blessed be. Live mythically. Keep sweet.

My PawPaw, H. Houston Groome, Sr., used to cleverly say (when he wanted to have visitors leave that stayed too long), "Charlotte, let's go to bed so these nice people can go home."

YINZ BE PURDY!!

James H. Groome

References

"There is something about jumping a horse over a fence, something that makes you feel good. Perhaps it's the risk, the gamble. In any event it's a thing I need." William Faulkner. As quoted in "Visit to Two-Finger Typist" by Elliot Chaze in LIFE magazine (14 July 1961). Retrieved from https://en.wikiquote.org/wiki/William_Faulkner. Wikiquote

Wells, K. (2019, January 23)."Plantain: A Healing Herb in your Backyard." Retrieved from https://wellnessmama.com/5387/plantain-healing-herb/

Mitchell, Monte. (October 22, 2009). Retrieved from https://www.journalnow.com/news/local/wilkesboro-s-most-haunted-hunting-for-ghosts-will-be-part/article_95befd4d-5247-57c7-8175-399bb03bb9ad.html

"The Story of Tom Dooley." (2019). Retrieved from http://ncvisitorcenter.com/Story_of_Tom_Dooley.html

Lee. (May 23, 2013). "The Tom Dooley Mystery." Retrieved from http://visitwilkesboronc.com/2013/05/23/the-tom-dooley-mystery/

"Great Smokey Mountains: Planting." (July 1, 2015). Retrieved from https://www.nps.gov/grsm/learn/historyculture/planting.htm

Wikipedia contributors. (2019, March 18). Blue Ridge Mountains. In Wikipedia, The Free Encyclopedia. Retrieved 20:20, April 8, 2019, from https://en.wikipedia.org/w/index.php?title=Blue_Ridge_Mountains&oldid=888399998

Mazzocchi, Jay. (2006) Caldwell County. Retrieved from https://www.ncpedia.org/geography/caldwell

Claggett, Stephen R. (Spring 1995) First Immigrants: Native American Settlers of North Carolina. Reprinted with permission from the Tar Heel Junior Historian. Retrieved from https://www.ncpedia.org/history/early/native-settlement

Alexander, Nancy. (1956). Here Will I Dwell: The Story of Caldwell County. Salisbury, NC: Rowan Print Company.

The Patterson School Foundation: About Us. Retrieved from https://pattersonschoolfoundation.org/about-us/

"Collett Leventhorpe." (2000, July 15). Retrieved from https://www.findagrave.com/memorial/11011/collett-leventhorpe

Randell Jones and North Carolina Daniel Boone Heritage Trail, Inc., "Beaver Creek," *Daniel Boone's Trail*, accessed May 6, 2019, http://bythewaywebf.webfactional.com/dboone/items/show/16?tour=1&index=6

Yadkin River Trail: North Carolina. (n.d.). Retrieved from https://www.traillink.com/trail/yadkin-river-trail/

Wikipedia contributors. (2019, March 29). Tom Dooley (song). In Wikipedia, The Free Encyclopedia. Retrieved 20:25, April 8, 2019, from https://en.wikipedia.org/w/index.php?title=Tom_Dooley_(song)&oldid=889952046

Curry, Peter J. (1998). " 'Tom Dooley': The Ballad That Started The Folk Boom." Retrieved from https://www.kingstontrioplace.com/tdooleydoc.htm#BOTTOM%20OF%20PAGE

Brown, Frank C. (1952). North Carolina Folklore. Volume II. Durham, NC. Duke University Press. Retrieved from https://archive.org/stream/frankcbrowncolle02fran/frankcbrowncolle02fran_djvu.txt

"The Story of Tom Dooley." (2019). Retrieved from http://ncvisitorcenter.com/Story_of_Tom_Dooley.html

The Scary Truth: The Legend of Tom Dooley. North Carolina Ghosts. Retrieved from https://northcarolinaghosts.com/mountains/tom-dooley/scary-truth/

Wikipedia contributors. (2019, April 16). Tom Dula. In Wikipedia, The Free Encyclopedia. Retrieved 15:44, May 19, 2019, from https://en.wikipedia.org/w/index.php?title=Tom_Dula&oldid=892705540

Wikipedia contributors. (2019, March 2). Arthur "Guitar Boogie" Smith. In Wikipedia, The Free Encyclopedia. Retrieved 10:46, April 10, 2019, from https://en.wikipedia.org/w/index.php?title=Arthur_%22Guitar_Boogie%22_Smith&oldid=885787891

The Brown Mountain Lights. North Carolina Ghosts. Retrieved from https://northcarolinaghosts.com/mountains/brown-mountain-lights/

Happy Valley Fiddler's Convention. (n.d.). Retrieved from https://happyvalleyfiddlers.org/

Wikipedia contributors. (2019, February 1). Doc Watson. In Wikipedia, The Free Encyclopedia. Retrieved 20:26, April 8, 2019, from https://en.wikipedia.org/w/index.php?title=Doc_Watson&oldid=881215274

Personal interview. Gregory Watson. February 27, 2019 by telephone.

Miller, Dan. (1998, July 30)."A Biography of Doc Watson." Flatpicking Guitar Magazine. Steve Carr, Editor. Retrieved from http://www.docsguitar.com/biography.html

Wikipedia contributors. (2019, January 6). Carl Story. In Wikipedia, The Free Encyclopedia. Retrieved 20:27, April 8, 2019, from https://en.wikipedia.org/w/index.php?title=Carl_Story&oldid=877066652

The Heritage Calendar 2019. Honorees 2014. Clyde "Pop" Ferguson Sr. and Clyde Ferguson, Jr. Retrieved from https://ncheritagecalendar.com/honorees/clyde-pop-ferguson-sr-and-clyde-ferguson-jr-2/

Blue Ridge Natural Heritage Area. "Clyde 'Pop' Ferguson." Retrieved from https://www.blueridgeheritage.com/artist/clyde-pop-ferguson/

Wikipedia contributors. (2018, May 15). Piedmont blues. In Wikipedia, The Free Encyclopedia. Retrieved 01:02, April 15, 2019, from https://en.wikipedia.org/w/index.php?title=Piedmont_blues&oldid=841300650

Piedmont Blues Preservation Society: Keeping the Blues Alive Since 1985. (2017). Retrieved from https://piedmontblues.org/

"Granite Falls To Host Art in the Park Concert." (May 8, 2014). Hickory Daily Record. Retrieved from https://www.hickoryrecord.com/news/granite-falls-to-host-art-in-the-park-concert/article_89f91c84-d62f-11e3-a374-0017a43b2370.html

Devores, Courtney. (May 5, 2014). Charlotte Observer. "Antiseen Guitarist Dies of Heart Attack." Retrieved from https://www.charlotteobserver.com/entertainment/article9119018.html

Blockbuster Presents Secrets of the Unknown: Bigfoot & Witches. "Episode 1: BIGFOOT." (1987, 1996) [VHS] Ft. Lauderdale, FL: Blockbuster Entertainment, Inc.

Bigfoot Field Researchers Organization BFRO. (2017). Retrieved from https://www.bfro.net/GDB/state_listing.asp?state=nc

"Fish Identification: Recommended Pond Species." (2018). North Carolina State University Department of Applied Ecology. Retrieved from https://appliedecology.cals.ncsu.edu/extension/fisheries/fish-identification/

Wikipedia contributors. (2019, March 11). Rock bass. In Wikipedia, The Free Encyclopedia. Retrieved 20:28, April 8, 2019, from https://en.wikipedia.org/w/index.php?title=Rock_bass&oldid=887219285

Jones, David Hunter. (October 28, 2009). Bass Slam. Profiling the Red Eye. Bassmaster. Retrieved from https://www.bassmaster.com/tips/bass-slam-profiling-redeye

Quinn, Steve. (August 24, 2012) "Hybrid Black Bass." Retrieved from https://www.in-fisherman.com/editorial/hybrid-black-bass/154884

"What Snake Is That?: North Carolina." (2017). Retrieved from http://www.whatsnakeisthat.com/category/region/southeast/north-carolina/

Mallory, Stephanie. (May 9, 2016). "Stop Killing Non-Venomous Snakes." Retrieved from https://www.realtree.com/the-realblog-with-stephanie-mallory/stop-killing-non-venomous-snakes

"Amphibians and Reptiles of North Carolina: Turtles." (2019). Retrieved from http://herpsofnc.org/turtles/

New tests find bee-killing pesticides in 51% of bee-friendly plants from garden centers across U.S. and Canada (online article). (2014). Friends of the Earth. Retrieved from https://foe.org/news/2014-06-new-tests-find-bee-killing-pesticides-in-51-percent-of-bee-friendly-plants/

Uyterhoeven, Sonia. (September 20, 2010). "Tip of the Week: Removing Invasive Japanese Stilt Grass." Plant Talk: Inside the New York Botanical Garden. Retrieved from https://www.nybg.org/blogs/plant-talk/2010/09/tip-of-the-week/tip-of-the-week-removing-invasive-japanese-stilt-grass/

Daltoni. (March 8, 2008). "Creecy Greens (and roadside produce stands)." Into the Woods. Retrieved from https://acornabbey.com/blog/?p=288

Chrisy. (9-27-18). "Red Eye Gravy." Homemade Hooplah. Retrieved from https://homemadehooplah.com/red-eye-gravy/

Photo Credits

Cover photo and Twin Poplars photo by Leila McMichael. Edited by Erin Pendley. Used with permission.

Map of Happy Valley. Leila McMichael. 2019. Used with permission.

Boone Pharmacy Almanac Calendar. 2019.

Indian Maiden Searching for Lost Lover on Brown Mountain. By Leila McMichael. 1969. Acrylic. Used with permission.

Fort Defiance. By Ken Thomas - KenThomas.us (personal website of photographer), Public Domain, https://commons.wikimedia.org/w/index.php?curid=3969392

Portrait of American General William Lenoir (1752-1839). By Johannes Oertel (1823–1909) - Archibald Henderson, The Conquest of the Old Southwest (New York: The Century Company, 1920), p. 182. Downloaded from Google Books, Full View., Public Domain, https://commons.wikimedia.org/w/index.php?curid=21392626
Creative Commons Legal Code. https://creativecommons.org/licenses/by-sa/2.5/legalcode

The original printing of the book cover has the only likeness of General Lenoir drawn from life, about 1830, artist, unfortunately, unknown. Given to the Fort Defiance Restoration by a great-great-great grandson, Dr. Howard Patterson, past President of the American College of Surgeons in 1969. *Fort Defiance and the General* by Margaret E. Harper. 1976. *Amazon.com*

Ferguson, King of the Mountain. Line art by Leila McMichael. 2019. Used with permission.

Official portrait of Astronaut Bill Lenoir posing in ejection escape suit (EES) holding helmet. By NASA - https://images.nasa.gov/details-S79-36440.html, Public Domain, https://commons.wikimedia.org/w/index.php?curid=510740

File:Unfinished portrait of Daniel Boone by Chester Harding 1820.jpg. (2013, December 30). Wikimedia Commons, the free media repository. Retrieved 14:33, May 6, 2019 from https://commons.wikimedia.org/w/index.php?title=File:Unfinished_portrait_of_Daniel_Boone_by_Chester_Harding_1820.jpg&oldid=112867252.
Creative Commons Legal Code. https://creativecommons.org/licenses/by-sa/2.5/legalcode

Cellu Products photos property of Jon Doll. Used with permission.

Artistic conception of Private Tom C. Dula with drum and fiddle. Line art by Leila McMichael. 2019. Used with permission. (Dula listed as a musician and a drummer on a muster roll per Wikipedia -- Wikipedia contributors. (2019, April 16). Tom Dula. In

Wikipedia, The Free Encyclopedia. Retrieved 11:21, May 31, 2019, from
https://en.wikipedia.org/w/index.php?title=Tom_Dula&oldid=892705540).

Late Winter. By James Houston Groome. 2017. Acrylic.

All fish pictures by angler, Jon Doll. Photo credits Jon Doll. Used with permission.

File:Lampropeltis getula getula.jpg. (2017, September 16). *Wikimedia Commons, the free media repository*. Retrieved 02:33, April 27, 2019
from https://commons.wikimedia.org/w/index.php?title=File:Lampropeltis_getula_getula.jpg&oldid=258756109.
Creative Commons Legal Code. https://creativecommons.org/licenses/by-sa/2.5/legalcode

File:Opossum 2.jpg. (2018, September 16). Wikimedia Commons, the free media repository.
Retrieved 02:38, April 27, 2019 from
https://commons.wikimedia.org/w/index.php?title=File:Opossum_2.jpg&oldid=320488423.
Creative Commons Legal Code. https://creativecommons.org/licenses/by-sa/2.5/legalcod

File:Honey bee on a dandelion, Sandy, Bedfordshire (7002893894).jpg. (2019, April 9).
Wikimedia Commons, the free media repository. Retrieved 14:06, April 27, 2019 from
https://commons.wikimedia.org/w/index.php?title=File:Honey_bee_on_a_dandelion,_Sandy,_Bedfordshire_(7002893894).jpg&oldid=345326558.
Creative Commons Legal Code. https://creativecommons.org/licenses/by-sa/2.5/legalcode

Suggested Reading

Appalachian Ghosts by Nancy Roberts with Photographs by Bruce Roberts. 1978

Fort Defiance and the General by Margaret E. Harper. 1976
> NOTE: The original printing of the book has the only likeness of General Lenoir drawn from life, about 1830, artist, unfortunately, unknown. Given to the Fort Defiance Restoration by a great-great-great grandson, Dr. Howard Patterson, past President of the American College of Surgeons in 1969. *Amazon.com*

Fly Fisherman of Caldwell County: North Carolina Life Stories by Ron Beane and Gretchen Griffith. 2015

Furnitureland by Nancy Alexander. 1990

Ghosts of the Yadkin Valley by R. G. Absher. 2009

Happy Valley, history and genealogy by Thomas Felix Hickerson. 1940

Here Will I Dwell: The Story of Caldwell County by Nancy Alexander. 1956

Images of America: Caldwell County by Michael C. Hardy. 2006

Lift Up Your Head, Tom Dooley: The True Story of the Appalachian Murder That Inspired One of America's Most Popular Ballads by John Foster West. 1993

Suggested Viewing

Blockbuster Presents Secrets of the Unknown: Bigfoot & Witches. "Episode 1: BIGFOOT." (1987, 1996) [VHS] Ft. Lauderdale, FL: Blockbuster Entertainment, Inc.

Caldwell Heritage Museum Presents A History of Caldwell County: "From a Wilderness to a Barn: From the early days to 1841." (2010) [DVD] Granite Falls, NC: Main Event Studios

Caldwell Heritage Museum Presents A History of Caldwell County: "From a Barn to a County Seat: From 1841 to 1861." (2011) [DVD] Granite Falls, NC: Main Event Studios

Caldwell Heritage Museum Presents A History of Caldwell County: "War and Reconstruction: From 1861 to 1870." (2012) [DVD] Granite Falls, NC: Main Event Studios

Caldwell Heritage Museum Presents A History of Caldwell County: "The Country Recovers: From 1870 to 1900." (2013) [DVD] Granite Falls, NC: Main Event Studios

Suggested Links

Visit Lenoir and NC Foothills.
https://explorecaldwell.com/
Click on the link to "Historic Happy Valley" under Featured Attractions

NC Pedia. "Fort Defiance"
https://www.ncpedia.org/fort-defiance

To find out more about NC historic signs, go to the North Carolina Highway Historical Marker Program (under NC Department of Cultural Resources) at http://www.ncmarkers.com/search.aspx and select Caldwell County, then type in the name you wish to research, such as Fort Defiance (which has the distinction of being NC 1) and Collett Leventhorpe, the two found in Happy Valley, or Stoneman's Raid and Davenport College, found in Lenoir, for example.

Other North Carolina historical markers, such as Laura Foster and Thomas C. Dula M-48 are found at
http://www.waymarking.com/cat/details.aspx?f=1&guid=cb4fa9b5-732a-47f0-a4ac-d2faa36e4b07&lat=35.912767&lon=-81.538617&t=6
　　　　Just scroll down, right click on and open in a new tab to read more about these markers.

The Ultimate Guide to Asheville & the Western North Carolina Mountains: The Online Version of the Best-selling Regional Guidebook. "Happy Valley"http://www.ashevilleguidebook.com/wnc/cultural-attractions/happy_valley.htm

The North Carolina Visitor Center. "The Story of Tom Dooley"
http://ncvisitorcenter.com/Story_of_Tom_Dooley.html

Notes

Made in the USA
Columbia, SC
19 June 2019